A PLEA

IN BEHALF OF

A CHRISTIAN NATION,

FOR THE

CHRISTIAN EDUCATION

OF ITS

YOUTH.

ADDRESSED TO VARIOUS CLASSES OF SOCIETY.

" ALL SOULS ARE MINE."

ABRIDGED FROM THE LARGER WORK OF

THE REV. GEORGE MONRO, M.A.

VICAR OF LETTERKENNY, IRELAND, IN THE YEAR 1711.

LONDON:

PRINTED FOR J. HATCHARD AND SON,
187, PICCADILLY;

AND MESSRS. J. AND A. ARCH, CORNHILL.

1823.

TO

MRS. FRY,

THE WELL-KNOWN

FRIEND

OF

EDUCATION AND REFORM

UPON

CHRISTIAN PRINCIPLES,

THIS BOOK IS DEDICATED,

WITH MUCH ESTEEM,

BY

HER FRIEND,

THE EDITOR.

CONTENTS.

———♦———

PART I.

CONTENTS.

PART II.

BIBLE LECTURES FOR YOUTH.

A

PLEA,

&c.

CHAPTER I.

Address to the true Patriot.

You wish well to your country; you wish the prosperity of states and kingdoms; and indeed it is no wonder that you should do so, for it is on the good or bad posture of affairs in them, that the temporal happiness or misery of mankind depends. Were the many dismal evils and calamities that abound in them, traced to their original, they would be found to spring from want of due care, and proper method, in the education of youth.

Some are ever crying out of injustice, others groaning under oppression; a third bemoaning the losses they have sustained by thefts and robberies: you will be informed of murders and perjuries, of rebellions and insurrections; you will observe that tricks, and cunning, and covetousness, that deceit and fraud, are found in all sorts of

B

trades, employments, and occupations. And to
what, I entreat you, can these and the like disorders,
which shake the peace and quiet, and undermine
the pleasure and advantages of civil society, be
more probably imputed than to this, that people
have not been betimes instructed in the principles
of religion, have not had their minds formed according to the precepts of Jesus Christ; have not been
taught the duties they owe their neighbour in every
capacity and station, nor trained up in the practice
of them from their younger years; have not been
acquainted with the moment and necessity of per-
forming the relative obligations of religion, nor with
the motives that enforce them; nor, in fine, have
been directed to desire earnestly that grace which
only can enable them to fulfil them? And what
wonder is it, if they who have never learned any
thing but the maxims of the world; who have
ever been under the dictates of flesh and blood;
who have never seen any thing in their parents
and teachers but immorality and vice, and a contempt of God and divine things, a stupid unconcern
for their souls; and who perhaps have been taught
to treat in ridicule all that is grave and serious,
just and sober, as mean and sneaking qualities;
what wonder is it if such proud knaves and rogues,
cheats and villains, in any trade, occupation, or
employment, they may happen to have the management of, if they scruple not the most criminal
and mischievous actions, when they may do them
with impunity; and if, when such as these drop
into any station, they manage it not for the benefit

of the public, but to serve the ends of their ambition and covetousness, their pride and revenge? These are the pests of the state, the plagues of society, and the troublers of the peace of mankind.

But, on the other hand, a virtuous and well-ordered education has a happy influence on the state in all its parts and concerns. It is this that sets pious and religious Princes on the throne, that fills our benches with just and impartial Judges, that puts men of candour and integrity in every station and employment, blesses every relation with persons well acquainted with the duties of it, and inclined to perform them. And in one word, it is this, that on the one hand makes magistrates to be men of public spirit, actuated not by mean and selfish, but generous and noble principles, that readily conceive and vigorously execute great and extensive designs and projects for the common good; that are zealous for God and his honour, encourage religion, assert its interests, honour and regard its votaries; that punish and chastise vice and immoralities, and will give no countenance to the abettors of irreligion and debauchery, but are a terror and discouragement to all sorts of evil doers; that will enact equitable and wholesome laws, and take care that they be impartially put in execution: these are they who reform abuses and corruptions, rescue the oppressed, and do speedy justice to the poor and needy. And on the other hand, it is this that renders the people manageable and submissive, peaceable and obedient;

not apt to murmur at every little inconvenience, but willing to put the most favourable construction on the actions of their superiors, and ready to assist and concur with them in whatever can tend to the benefit of the public.

These are some of the blessed advantages that result from a pious education, with respect to the state. They who have been bred up from their infancy in the fear and love of God, and so are become habitually good and virtuous, will adorn every station and profession, recommend every trade and occupation, and even render them public blessings and great benefits. These are the most useful and the most profitable members of the state, its strongest supports as well as its greatest ornaments, and who, either by their piety prevent God's judgments, or, by their standing in the gap, avert them when they are deserved and impending; the blessed God being used, for their sakes, to spare an otherwise sinful nation. Wherefore it is the duty as well as the interest of all, to endeavour by all possible means, to advance a concern that is attended with consequences so happy and so advantageous.

" Happy is the nation that is exalted by righteousness!

" Yea, happy is the people whose God is the Lord!"

CHAPTER II.

Address to Persons of Quality.

You whom God in his kind providence hath raised up to honour and greatness, and distinguished by peculiar instances of his bounty; from you it is but reasonable that he should expect becoming returns and acknowledgments; and there is nothing whereby you can express more acceptably the grateful sense you have of his favours, than to discover the great regard you have for his religion, by practising its excellent precepts—first in your own persons, and then by using your power and influence, to recommend it to those who have any dependence upon you.

The examples of superiors have in them a charming force, that constrains those under their dependence to imitate their practice.

You cannot but be sensible how sacred your obligations are, to be patterns of piety in every capacity you bear.

The advantages which attend your being such, are very signal; they are not confined to your own persons and families, but redound to others, who are gained to become votaries to religion by your illustrious examples.

The great and eminent privileges and blessings which accompany a serious piety with regard to yourselves, cannot but infinitely recommend it to you. It will add lustre to your other qualities, it will adorn your conversation, heighten your breeding, and grace all your accomplishments. It will adorn and perfect your souls; for, what more noble and more valuable ornaments, than to be meek and humble; to be pure, and chaste, and self-denied; to be modest and gentle, patient and contented, just and charitable, spiritual and heavenly-minded, compassionate and merciful? It is in these that the beauty and perfection of the inward man consists. And further, it will rescue you from ignoble and base-born lusts, and make you partakers of the Divine Nature; it will beget serenity in your minds, and peace in your consciences, afford you solid pleasures, and entitle you to durable riches; it will turn you away from the love and esteem of earthly things, and raise your minds to the contemplation and desire of more noble and more excellent objects, even eternal realities: you will then look down with a generous disdain, on the pleasures of flesh and sense, and the glories of this world, as things vastly unworthy of your first notice and your principal pursuit. In a word, by it you will become the members of Christ and his living images, the favourites of heaven and the heirs of glory; the care of angels, and the joy of saints; and unite with them in their heavenly employ of love, praise, and adoration; and, in fine, you shall improve and grow in those blessed dispositions which will qualify you for entering on the undefiled inheritance, and for relishing the joys of the other world.

And thus your own experience will effectually convince you, that the pleasures of a religious and devout life are not imaginary and fantastic, as the profane world would give it out; but solid, real, and well-grounded, and such as infinitely transcend those sordid and despicable satisfactions which the votaries of debauchery and vice are so fond of, which are attended with disquietudes, and shall end in sorrow; leaving the forlorn soul nothing to inherit, but its vicious and perverted dispositions, the only things that accompany it into the other world.

Your experience of the life and power of true piety and the joys of devotion, will give you more solid and permanent assurance both of the being of God, and of the truth and excellency of the Christian religion, than all that can be obtained by the methods of speculation, and such as all the wit and sophistry of atheists shall never be able to shake or elude.

Now, as true goodness is communicative, and tends to reproduce itself; so, when once you are practically acquainted with religion, when its sacred principles are vitally and habitually rooted in your hearts, and, as it were, interwoven with your natures,

it will powerfully incline you to endeavour the pro-
pagation of it every where, and more especially
among your offspring, those future hopes of your
noble and honourable families, to whom you cannot possibly give more eminent and more endearing instances of your love, than to consecrate them
betimes to God, to disciple them unto their Redeemer, by acquainting them, as soon as may be,
with the maxims, and by initiating them into the
practices of the Christian religion; to labour, by
your pious instructions, by your fervent prayers and
virtuous example, that they may become new creatures, and be made partakers of the Divine Nature;
for, by so doing, you will be instrumental to entail
upon them a more glorious inheritance, and a nobler
birth, than what they derive from yourselves; because
to be born of God, and to be joint heirs with
Jesus Christ, excels inconceivably all that the
world calls great and magnificent. O! how vast
a satisfaction will it afford you, to see your children constrained by the love of Jesus, transcribing
his example, deserving his grace, and still aspiring
after greater conformity to him in every thing; to
see them despising the maxims of the world, and
trampling on the momentary vanities of this life,
and fixing on the glories of the other world, as
their portion and their inheritance! Then it is,
that they shall be " as olive plants round about
your tables," shedding forth the savour of gracious
dispositions, and an agreeable conversation; and
at last become public blessings, and the great ornaments and pillars of the nation.

But the happy consequences of your piety are not limited to your own families, but reach all that are round about you ; for, when others observe that you, who have the greatest advantages of gratifying all the inclinations and appetites of flesh and blood, do notwithstanding embrace the strictness of religion, and prefer the pleasures of devotion to the satisfactions of sense, they are powerfully invited to try the experiment, and to write after your copy. Your conspicuous piety will not only lay restraints upon, shame, and dash profaneness and irreligion, but also secretly draw those that converse with you, to cast a favourable eye on a holy life. But your zeal and charity will not let you rest in merely exemplifying a serious piety ; they will moreover push you, when a seasonable juncture offers, to speak honourably of it, and to assert it against the attacks of profane and atheistical wits, to discountenance a vicious and sensual life, and to represent it as it is, a reproach to human nature, as a dishonour to the Christian religion. And among the many other excellent dispositions which a vital piety will beget in your hearts, it will inspire you with warm love to, and tender concern for, the souls of men ; whence you will be prompted to contribute whatever you can, for the promoting of their eternal salvation, and consequently to employ all your interest that Christian piety may be encouraged and promoted every where, and among all persons, and that none want the means and advantages of becoming devout and virtuous, so far as your influence can reach it; and especially that the young may be timely acquainted with religion: this being a concern of the greatest moment, cannot but go very near your hearts, and incline you to concur with your best assistance for advancing it. Now, it is certain that the influence of your quality and superiority, especially when it is rendered venerable by your own personal piety, and recommended by the happy effects it has produced in your noble families, has a very powerful tendency that way. The great deference you pay to religion in all its concerns, the tender regard you have for God and for his honour, your remarkable diligence and care to instruct your children in the knowledge of Christianity, your abhorrence of immorality and injustice; these, I say, and all other instances of your piety and goodness, are very powerful inducements to your servants and dependents, to write after the fair copy you set before them, and the rather, when they observe that you put peculiar marks of your favour on the good and virtuous, and that you discountenance and even punish the vicious and profligate.

In short, it evidently appears that your state and circumstances in this world, put you in a capacity and give you many excellent advantages and opportunities of doing good, that others in a lower rank cannot pretend to; and you may be confident that the more zealously you employ your power and greatness, in encouraging and promoting the interests of religion and virtue among those that are within the reach of your influence, as it will render you truly more illustrious and observable than a noble birth or vast possessions can do, so it will more certainly entitle you to, and secure for you, the solid and permanent glories of eternity.

CHAPTER III.

Address to Masters of Schools, Tutors, and Governors.

THE bringing up children according to the spirit and customs of the world, is not the Education I am recommending.   No: it is one of a more noble strain and of higher aims; it is that which the Christian Religion directs and prescribes; an Education that is managed according to the spirit and maxims, the doctrine and example of the Redeemer: this is the mould, according to which they must be fashioned, the lovely pattern which they should be taught to imitate and conform to.

And here I must beg leave to speak with freedom, and open my thoughts to you, under whose conduct and inspection they are commonly trained.

These future hopes of church, and state, and families, these candidates for heaven, these dear pledges of their parents, these lambs of Jesus Christ, are very early committed to your trust and care; you have the management of them in their younger and more flexible years; in the prime and flower of their age, when they are most capable of good impressions. You may, by the grace and blessing of God, be happily instrumental to engage them to become the early votaries of religion and a holy life, if you will but piously improve the advantages you have to influence them, especially when they see that your address them affectionately, and urge the great things of religion on them with constancy and seriousness.

Though parents commonly, when they put their children to school, do very little mind or design their Christian education; the attainment of human learning being that which they principally purpose, and aim at; yet I cannot understand how you can be excused (from being highly criminal) before God, if you do not heartily endeavour to improve the youth committed to your charge, by acquainting them by times with the principles of Christianity, and guiding them, to the best of your skill, in the practices of a solid piety. You ought to consider that it is not so much the parents, as God in his providence that puts them under your care and tuition. And, therefore, you should look on them as so many talents wherewith he hath intrusted you, and for which he will reckon with you one day, and will reward you according to the improvements you have made of them. Your diligence in teaching them the languages, how indefatigable soever it may be, and though even you should perfectly accomplish them, both in that and in all other parts of human learning, will be of no consideration in the sight of God, if you should neglect improving their nobler faculties and seasoning them with the maxims of religion and virtue; for, to be sure, whatever designs the parents may have, yet God intends that they should be trained up for another world, and put as soon as may be in the way that leads to life and immortality. Therefore, though the parents may perhaps reward you for answering their designs, yet you cannot justly hope to be rewarded by God, since you have either not at all, or but very superficially, endeavoured to fulfil his gracious intentions. And, alas! what a melancholy reflection is it, that one should spend so much of his time and pains, exhaust his strength and vigour, in doing that for which he has no reasonable ground to hope that he will be recompensed in a better world; and pray, when we consider things impartially, what other reckoning can be made of all your toil and labour, in acquainting the youth that are committed to your trust with the monuments of Paganism, and the antiquities of Greece and Rome, and filling their heads with dry and lean criticisms, or with the absurd and very often impure fictions of the poets: what reckoning, I say, can be made of all this diligence, if all the while no regard be had to the one thing necessary; but that it is a vain, unprofitable, and even hurtful spending of precious time? I cannot for my heart hinder myself from believing, but that some unhappy tincture, secretly disposing to irreligion and profaneness, is derived into the hearts of the youth from a too early perusal of the pagan writings, especially such as commonly obtain in schools, and before they are sufficiently fortified against the infection, by being solidly established in the principles of Christianity. O how deplorable a loss is it, that the children of Christian parents, solemnly devoted to the service of the Lord Jesus, and therefore inviolably obliged to give him the first fruits of their time, and thoughts, and affections, should, even under the conduct of Christian schoolmasters, be in the very morning of their age initiated into the mysteries of Paganism! For I reckon that so they are in a sort, when more time and pains by far is employed in teaching them the rites and ceremonies, the worship, and gods, and customs of the pagan world, and giving them the sense and meaning of its authors, than in teaching them the precepts, and acquainting them with the life and sufferings, of their Redeemer. Can the Father of spirits, think you, take it well, that his own offspring, whom he designed for the fruition of himself and of his divine joys; and commands all that instruct them, to breed them up with a continual regard to this end, and to begin in the bloom of youth the improvement of their nobler capacities, by a pious and devout remembrance of their Creator : can he, I say, take it well, that his offspring, whom he so dearly loves, should receive their first impressions from the impure and muddy sources of heathenism, and be better acquainted with the worship, and sacrifices, and genealogy of false deities, than with his own nature and perfections, and the ways of worshipping him acceptably? Will not the charitable Redeemer of mankind highly resent that those precious souls for whom he paid so invaluable a ransom, and who he intends should be the co-heirs of his glory, are not more carefully looked after, are not better instructed in the mysteries of his religion, and have not hearty endeavours used, to form them according to the lovely pattern that he left for their imitation, both in his life and death?

O the unspeakable prejudice and hurt that must infallibly redound to youth, by this way of procedure; to shuffle out the only necessary and most important concerns, the concerns of their souls and their salvation, from having any share of their time and pains, and to educate them so as to make them believe that the attainment of languages and learning is the very scope and end of their creation, and that they are not capable of nobler endowments!

What other construction can they put on the strict injunctions that are given them, to ply their books, the constant attendance that is required of them to that end, the severity wherewith their negligence is punished, and the continual application of thought which they are obliged to exercise late and early, night and day; what can they think, since no other thing is urged on them with so much solemnity and earnestness, but that these things that are so recommended, are the most necessary and important, and that any thing else is not to be put in the balance with them? And what is all this, but deplorably to mismanage their education? How infinitely more reasonable in itself, as well as more profitable for the youth, would it be, to employ some just proportions of their time in conversing with them about serious matters; in setting before them the beauties and excellencies of religion; giving them true notions of it, and guarding them against immorality and vice; acquainting them with their souls, with the happiness that is designed for them, and with the ways that lead to it; and finally, representing to them the glorious advantages and unspeakable comforts of a pious and devout life. How unaccountable is it, that in places where education is pretended to be the main design, these things are not more insisted on; nay, that they are not made the great and chief employment, both of masters and pupils! Why should not other things come in, rather by way of recreation, than as the principal mark and scope at which their studies should be levelled? Is it not a subversion of the designs of God, an acting contrary to the spirit and dignity of religion and the true interest of souls, when matters are otherwise ordered? Will human learning advance the less prosperously, or the youth incur any prejudice, if the things of God and eternity have the precedency, or even the choicest portions of their time and thoughts? Is not this the way to sanctify their studies, and to render them solidly learned? Which are the most noble accomplishments; to have the soul adorned with early piety and devotion, and with the Christian graces, or to be an expert grammarian, rhetorician, logician, or whatever else you can imagine? What is it that most effectually improves the mind, and ennobles its faculties and powers; to be excited and directed betimes to the desire, love, and contemplation of God, that infinitely amiable Being, the original and the end, the Father of spirits, and the fountain of happiness; or to the desire and love of

C

sciences, very often falsely so called, which rather puff up, than give solid and real satisfaction to the soul? And is it not most equitable, that as the former, being the most excellent and valuable things, deserve the pre-eminence in their affections, so they should have the prime and first fruits, yea, the largest share of their time and thoughts allotted them? It is left to the candid and serious to determine, whether or not there be any just ground for such expostulations as these : I wish with all my heart that I were mistaken, and that things were otherwise than I have represented them.

In the mean time, it is, I think, evident to a demonstration, that you cannot pretend to discharge faithfully, the great trust committed to you, nor justly hope to be able to account for it with joy at the great day, if you do not to the best of your skill, and with the greatest care and diligence possible, apply yourselves to form the youth according to the maxims of the Gospel. To do this, without doubt, is the great design of the station you are in. Other things are but subordinate ends. You are indeed, by virtue of your function, obliged to instruct the youth under your inspection in the languages, and such other things as may qualify them for being useful members of the state. But then you must take heed that an eager prosecution of these lesser things do not engross your time and pains, to the prejudice and disadvantage of the more excellent and more necessary concerns. You should remember, as has been already intimated, that they are designed to be citizens of another world, and therefore that your principal study must be how to fit them for the employments of that blessed state. This is that noble and worthy end you should propose to yourselves in their education, and at which all your endeavours should more especially aim; and that you may happily attain to it, as you ought yourselves to be well instructed in, and have a deep and serious sense of the great things of the Christain religion, so you must be at pains to convey them into the hearts of the youth: you must, for instance, with zeal and affection, and in humble dependence on the influences and conduct of the divine grace, begin early to acquaint them with their Redeemer, teach them to know " Jesus Christ, and him crucified:" you must set before them the example of his holy life, his cross, his sufferings and death, and seriously recommend conformity to him in all things: you must train them up in the love of self-denial, contempt of the world, and resignation to the will of God, and carefully represent to them the excellency, delightfulness, and necessity of these practices. You must inform them of the strait gate and narrow way; that is, the way of the cross, of sufferings and mortification, and make them sensible that it is a lovely way, a way that is full of pleasure and peace, and that leads infallibly unto life eternal. You must solidly convince them of the great corruption and degeneracy of human nature, and of the necessity of the Spirit and grace of Jesus Christ, in order to enlighten, purify, and heal the dark, unclean, and diseased souls of men. You must guard them against the spirit and maxims, the courses and practices of the wicked world, and carefully suppress in them the love and desire of ease and pleasure, of riches and fulness, of honour and greatness, representing them as very unsuitable to a state wherein they must watch and labour, run and wrestle, fight and strive, in order to recover their heavenly country. You must, in fine, disparage and expose the corrupt inclinations, lusts, and passions of depraved nature, as their mortal and bosom enemies, which they must resolve to overcome and exterminate, before they can be crowned with the glories of eternity. In a word, your work is to disciple them to the holy Jesus, and to lead them to trace the footsteps of their dear Redeemer; to conform to so divine a pattern in every thing; to learn of him to be meek and lowly in heart, and to take his yoke upon them, and so they shall find rest for their souls. This it is to educate youth according to the principles of the Gospel.

But perhaps some may imagine, that I impose too much upon you, and that I would have you invade the pastoral office; that it is the province of those that are invested with it, to teach divinity; and that, for your parts, you have task enough in teaching the languages, and other parts of learning, though you be not burdened with the additional charge of looking after souls. To this it is answered, that though it be the peculiar charge of pastors to teach and recommend the truths and duties of religion, yet certainly to do so is in some sort the duty of all, as occasion offers, and they have abilities for it. It is true, all are not to take upon themselves public and authoritative teaching, that being reserved for those that are devoted and set apart for that end; yet, since instructing the ignorant is one great instance of that charity that is due to the souls of men, I do not see how any serious Christian that competently understands the principles of his religion, can be excused from it. The great Apostle, in several passages of his Epistles, enjoins all the faithful to teach and admonish one another (Col. iii. 16); to exhort one another daily (Heb. iii. 13), and to provoke to love and good works. Yea, even the other sex are not exempted from this obligation: for the same Apostle expressly requires, that the aged women be teachers of good things (Tit. ii. 3, 4), and particularly that they instruct the young women in those Christian virtues that belong to their age and station, that adorn their sex, and recommend their holy profession. But besides, there are some relations which indispensably oblige to this. Thus, for instance, parents are obliged to bring up their children in the nurture and admonition of the Lord; husbands are obliged to instruct their wives, and masters their servants. It was Abraham's goodly character, that for which God did especially take notice of him, that he commanded not only his children but his household, to keep the ways of the Lord, and to do justice and judgment (Gen. xviii. 19). And accordingly we may observe what notable discoveries of piety

and devotion his servant Eleazer gave in discharging
his embassy, when sent to procure a wife for Isaac;
in which we have not only a proof that he had
been religiously educated, but also the happy consequences of his being so; to wit, great fidelity
and diligence, and a pious dependence on the
divine conduct, in managing what had been committed to his trust. Now it would be very strange,
if the masters of schools were under no engage-
ment to instruct their scholars in the principles
of Christianity. Certainly the relation that you
have to the youth is very considerable; it gives
you the greatest advantages and the fairest opportunities imaginable, to advance the good of souls;
and not to make use of them for that end, would
be an unpardonable neglect. Your scholars are
commonly put under your conduct and inspection,
when they are very young, when they are ductile and
pliable; and many of them at least are capable of
being cast into what mould you will. Your authority over them is very great, and they stand in awe
of it; and when you manage it with prudence and
discretion, when you take care that it is not soured,
nor rendered frightful and unacceptable, by exces-
sive roughness and severities, but recommended
by methods of love and sweetness, you may issue
out what orders you please, they will meet with
a cheerful compliance; and your very chastisements,
when they begin to observe that they proceed
from love, and that it is with unwillingness you
thus afflict them, will at last be meekly submitted
to, and they will love you even when you correct

them, because they see that it is not humour, or passion that influences you in inflicting these strokes, but a real design to advance their good, and to prevent their miscarrying. I know that the tempers of children are very different, and that consequently different methods must be taken in dealing with them. But then I doubt not but an authority which is exercised with a prudent love and an obliging sweetness, will be found the most effectual way to melt and reduce the most stubborn and rebellious spirit, which, however, does not hinder but just severities may be used, when it is absolutely necessary so to do. And when all this is considered, is it not very reasonable, nay, is it not your indispensable duty, to employ the advantages with which the relation you bear to the youth furnishes you, chiefly in gaining them to the love of God, and to the practices of religion? They are obliged to remember their Creator in the days of their youth; and how can they do so, unless they are taught that it is their duty, and what it imports? They continue for several years under your care and tuition; and if they do not learn the principles of religion in that space of time, a good part of their youth is spent very unprofitably, in forgetfulness of God, and a profound ignorance of the only necessary and most valuable things. Some of them are at a distance from their parents, and such as are near to them, are obliged to give you constant attendance; so that though they would, yet they cannot, but you may when, and as often as you please, discourse with them about their spiritual concerns. You can appoint what hours, and prescribe what tasks you think proper, in order to promote their Christian education; you can call them to give an account of their diligence, and inquire into their progress; you can know their capacities, and accordingly suit your instructions: in a word, you can do them a thousand good offices that none else can, and have many ways to influence them, that others cannot pretend to; and therefore what a loss would it be, if the notable advantages and occasions which you have for improving them in goodness and virtue, should not be directed to the attainment of so justly valuable an end, and in comparison whereof, all the other kindnesses and services you can do them, are but of very small moment.

As to the pastors, if any of you should be so weak as to make use of so absurd a pretence, (which, indeed, I can scarcely believe), I dare undertake that they will not consider your care to instruct the youth committed to your trust, in the truths of the Christian religion, and to guide and exhort them to the practices of a holy life, as an encroachment on their functions; nay, on the contrary, I am very confident, that they will not only highly approve your conduct, but heartily encourage it, assist you in it with their best advice, and as often as they can, take the task off your hands, for they know that their Lord and Master, that great and chief Shepherd of the sheep, hath expressly given a commission to feed his lambs. And therefore, to be sure, *they* will not neglect to look after them ; but in imitation of the great Shepherd, they will gather them with their arms, and carry them in their bosoms. They will treat them with the greatest tenderness and affection, and labour to advance them from the state of babes in Christ, to that of perfect men ; and that not by drily and transiently proposing a few questions now and then, which could only beget some faint and ineffectual notions of Divine things in their heads ; but by frequently and seriously addressing their young hearts, in order to excite them to the love of God, to fervent desires after his love and grace, and to pious resolutions of obeying his precepts ; so that *they* are your fellow-labourers in this great affair. In effect, the business of a Christian education being a matter of infinite consequence and moment, God hath so ordered it in his good providence, that persons of different stations and characters are engaged to interest themselves in advancing it. Pastors and parents, schoolmasters and teachers of all sorts, are under indispensable obligations to carry it on with all their might.

Your task, I must own, is very great, and full of toil and labour ; but then it is very honourable, and the issue will be glorious both to yourselves and to those under your care. It is certainly a great honour, that by your pains and endeavours, so many of the youth are fitted to become profitable members of society, and made capable of bearing the most important posts and stations. But O! how vastly greater is it, to be the instruments that God makes use of to dress their souls for the glories of the other world, to add to the number of the blessed, to augment the inhabitants of the heavenly Jerusalem, and to furnish such as shall celebrate the praises of God for ever! O how vast a satisfaction, how solid a pleasure will you feel, when your consciences tell you, that from a principle of love to God, and sincere intentions to advance his gracious designs on mankind, you have used your best endeavours, and all the art and skill you were masters of, to gain early votaries to religion, and to rescue such of their precious souls for whom Christ died, as were under your inspection, from the slavery of corruption and sin, and to engage them to become the soldiers and servants of their Redeemer, and manfully to fight under his banners against all their spiritual enemies. What good ground have you to hope, that that blessed recompense mentioned by the prophet Daniel will be one day conferred on you; " they that be wise shall shine as the brightness of the firmament, and they that turn many to righteousness as the stars for ever and ever." The truly wise are only those who are truly religious. " Behold, the fear of the Lord, that is wisdom: and to depart from evil, that is understanding." And wherever true religion is, as I observed before, it inspires with noble designs and charitable projects for the good of mankind. And because the greatest good that can be done them, is to prevent their sin and misery, by engaging them in the practices of a righteous and holy life; therefore, all good souls bend their endeavours more especially that way; and God, to encourage such charitable attempts, hath promised that he will gloriously reward them in a better world. Now I reckon that your pious diligence to reform the manners of the youth whereof you have the charge, and to season their hearts betimes with the maxims of piety, to train them up in the love of God, and in the exercise of the Christian graces, and so to introduce them happily into the paths that lead to bliss, is really to turn many to righteousness, and that consequently it entitles you to the promised reward which will infallibly be given you, when the solemn day of the distribution of rewards shall come. And the more heroic and indefatigable your efforts are, when the love of Jesus is the principle whence they proceed, and the happiness of those souls for whom he shed his precious blood, the end at which they aim, the more eminent and illustrious will the degrees of glory be, to which you shall be advanced in another world.

CHAPTER IV.

Address to the female Instructors of Youth.

You, my respected friends, are under the same obligations that schoolmasters and governors are, to
train up those you have the charge of, in the fear of
God. You have the same advantages of authority,
and of young and flexible minds. You are as indispensably obliged to be teachers of good things as
they are : your negligence in this great affair will be
as criminal as theirs, and the consequences of your
diligence are very important, and most beneficial to
mankind ; for it is by your serious exhortations and
pious endeavours, in a great measure, that the
younger women should be taught how to fulfil the
weighty and momentous obligations of those several relations which they may have occasion to bear in
the different stations of life. Every one knows, that
as a prudent, discreet, and Christian behaviour in
these relations hath a singular tendency to promote
the welfare and happiness of families, so their mis-
conduct in them is a source of manifold evils and
most afflicting calamities. Now the only effectual
way to prevent these miseries, and to procure the contrary blessings, is to take care that they be brought
up under the influences of religion ; that they be
acquainted betimes with the principles of Christianity, and initiated into the exercises of devotion,
and the practice of solid virtue and goodness ; and

when religion is become habitual to them, it will easily form itself into all the duties, which the several relations and states they may be engaged in will call for; (wherefore you are strictly obliged, while they are under your conduct, to use your utmost endeavours to persuade and win them to an early piety, in doing which you will be the happy instrument of procuring to the world a great deal of good; for) a young woman that has been piously educated, will be a singular blessing and an honour to the family into which she enters. Her exemplary virtues will diffuse and spread themselves through all the members.

" She openeth her mouth with wisdom, and in her tongue is the law of kindness; she looketh well to the ways of her household, and eateth not the bread of the idleness: her children arise up, and call her blessed; her husband also, and he praiseth her." Whatever may be her state of life, her fragrant virtues, her serious and undissembled devotion, will invite all that converse with her, to the love and imitation of them.

You will consider, my friends, that there are some graces so peculiarly the ornaments of the female sex, that they ought to appear in them, in a very conspicuous manner; such as divine love, and a fervent devotion, meekness and modesty, purity and chastity, mercifulness and humility; and these you should with all possible care inculcate, and tell them that without these, whatever advantages, of either beauty, or birth, or breeding, or natural accomplishments, they may have, yet they will make a contemptible figure in the sight of God and of good men. These are the things that make up the dress in which their souls should be invested; these are the jewels, and pearls, and gold, that must grace and beautify the hidden man of the heart; these are the ornaments that render them truly lovely, and that will lead them to the noblest title, " Sons and daughters of the Lord Almighty!"

When you are apparelling their bodies, you should take occasion to inform them, that they have nobler and more valuable parts, which they should be more solicitous to adorn; show them the danger of being so scrupulously nice about the garb of their outward man, and yet patiently bear with the irregularities of their minds, and never use any hearty endeavours to redress them; and that they should so anxiously study, by neatness and outward ornaments, to recommend themselves to the eyes of men, and take no care, by purity and devotion, to please the Searcher of hearts! Such pious reflections may be very useful, with God's blessing, to excite good thoughts and serious inclinations in them; for, being taken from objects that are familiar to them, they are proper to convey with ease the sense of divine things into their minds.

The main things of religion may be made plain and suited even to the capacities of children, and the wayfaring man, though a fool, shall not err therein; and how weak soever his capacities may otherwise be, he will understand so much of them as is necessary for the government of his life, and to guide him safe to heaven.

CHAPTER V.

Prayer against vain Thoughts.

Lord, wilt thou so wonderfully condescend as to take up with so mean a dwelling as my heart, and shall I leave it open to thine enemies, shall I admit there what my Lord abhorreth? Wilt thou dwell in my heart, and shall I suffer thoughts of pride, or lust, or malice, to enter in or dwell with thee? Are these, Lord, fit companions for the Spirit of thy grace? I know I must part with them, or lose the sweet influence of thy grace, and shall I drive away so dear a friend?

Lord, I know there is no true cure for sinful, vain, unprofitable thoughts, but by consecrating the heart entirely to thy love and service, who hast by the wonders of thy love so well deserved it. Lord, do thou enter into my heart; keep it as thy own; drive out the buyers and sellers, and make it an house of prayer!

Lord, can we want matter for our thoughts, when we have thee, our life, our hope, our happiness, to think of? Lord, let us love thee strongly, that we may never forget thee; we shall then see thee in every thing that meets us, and hear thee in every one that speaketh to us. Lord, if thou art not in all our thoughts, it is because thou art not in our hearts. Lord, we have the glories of thy nature, the wonders of thy love, to think upon; thy law to meditate in; and heaven and glory to fill our souls.

CHAPTER VI.

Christian Parents.

IF indeed your children were creatures of time, and designed only for the enjoyments of this life, it were reasonable that they should be wholly educated according to its maxims; but seeing they are born to the hopes of a better world, it is but just that they should be trained up in the knowledge and practice of those things which qualify for the enjoyments and employments of that future happy state.

The men of this world, whose designs and contrivances for their children rise no higher than the things of time, are very careful to have them bred in those ways of living which may yield them riches, honours, and pleasures: and shall not Christians, who profess and believe that there is a state of never-ending bliss and glory to be enjoyed in another world, and that this life is, and indeed ought to be considered as such by all, a time of preparation for it, shall not they be infinitely more concerned to have their children made meet and fitted for an " inheritance incorruptible, undefiled, and that fadeth not away ?"   Alas! shall the children of this world be in this respect wiser than the children of light ?   How unaccountable is it, that eternity, and the things of it, should so little influence the education of youth; and that the world, with its empty trifles and momentary vanities, should engage the whole of it; should engross, devour, and swallow up all the time of their life; and especially the more precious moments of it, their blooming years, the days of health and vigour, which God hath expressly ordered should be consecrated to the remembrance of himself? "The teaching them a little Latin and Greek," as a judicious author observes, "how much soever those noble languages may conduce to polite literature, would not deserve the name of Christian education, were not at the same time the greatest regard paid to the subduing of disorderly passions, the rectifying of perverse inclinations, the planting of virtuous habits, and the securing them by religious principles."

CHAPTER VII.

Address to negligent Parents.

To you belongs this awful confession: Most of all the evils which we see and feel are owing to our own remissness and negligence, and because we do not labour to form our children to piety in their tender years. We are at the pains to cause them to be instructed in profane arts and sciences; we use all possible endeavours to procure for them considerable employments at court and in the armies; we heap up wealth for them, and provide them friends; in fine, we do our utmost to make them considerable in the world; but we take no care to procure for them the favour and love of the King of angels, nor to endeavour their advancement into an honourable station in the court of heaven. But, alas! have not your children souls as well as bodies? And do you not confess the one to be divine and immortal, the other earthly and perishing? If to provide for the necessities and conveniencies of the outward man, is all the duty you owe your children, what difference do you make between them and your beasts? for you take care that even they be well accommodated, in whatever is necessary for the support of their animal life; and if you do no more for your children than this, you plainly intimate that you intend they should live no other life than that of beasts, and consequently that they should enjoy no other rewards, but such as suit and agree with a brutish and sensual life. But the great pretence, by which careless parents think to wipe off the dreadful charge of being accessory to the destruction of their children, is, that they send them to schools and colleges, and commit them to the care and inspection of others, who are better qualified to teach and instruct their children than they themselves are; and besides, that the ministers of religion are especially obliged to interest themselves in this weighty concern, being, by virtue of their office, the watchmen of the souls both of old and young. To this I answer, that it is extremely to be wished, that schools and colleges were nurseries of piety as well as of human learning; and that the masters and governors of these societies were not only professors of languages and philosophy, but eminent patterns of Christianity also. It is certain, that such they ought to be, and that it is their duty to look very narrowly to the spiritual concerns of the youth committed to their care; and that God will sadly reckon with them for the neglect of this most necessary and most indispensable part of their province. Of this it may be said, that as the design of the parents in sending their children to these seminaries is not, that they may become Christians, but that they may become accomplished in the languages and the wisdom of this world; so the masters fully gratify them in this, and bend the whole of their endeavours to instruct the youth intrusted to their inspection in human arts and sciences. This is the mark they aim at; piety and its concerns come in only by the by. When the weightier affairs of languages, philosophy, and the mathematics, are over (the former take up near the whole of the time both of masters and disciples, the latter only some small shreds and parcels of it), the one is vigorously set about, the other but very superficially and triflingly handled; as if it were by far the least essential and momentous concern!

CHAPTER VIII.

Answers to Objections against a Christian Education.

THERE are some that object, that notwithstanding all the endeavours that are used to educate the youth piously, yet many of them continue vicious, and several, even of those who have gone from under the conduct of their instructors with very good dispositions, have degenerated and become irreligious and profligate; and, therefore, that it is needless to be at such pains to acquaint them with religion; that these serious matters will come in more seasonably when the follies of childhood and the heat and fervour of youth are over; when they have attained to sedateness of thought and maturity of judgment, and are more apt to listen to wholesome counsels.

At this rate of arguing, the Gospel itself must be discarded; since, alas! there are too many that continue wicked and profane, notwithstanding the great advantages they enjoy by it.

Parents and teachers are not to give over because they have not absolute and infallible assurances of success; it is enough for their encouragement that they have a hopeful prospect, and that God has promised to reward their pious endeavours with his blessing.

The instructors of youth should not be discouraged, nor think that all is lost, because they do not see the fruits of their care to appear with that speed that they could wish.

Though the effects of a religious education do not presently appear, yet it has been observed, that the principles of piety which have been dropt into the hearts of some while they were young, have afterwards, in a divine and fertile soil, sprung up into the practice of a holy life; and many who had declined from the good dispositions that were wrought in them by the care of pious parents and teachers, and led a vicious and debauched life, have seriously acknowledged, that the sense they had of their virtuous education did often check and restrain them, when they were in the career of gratifying their lusts, and at last, with God's blessing, proved the mean of recovering them into the paths of wisdom and sobriety. Let pious teachers still continue their endeavours; and even when they can endeavour no more, because the youth are no longer under their inspection, they should continue to water all that they have planted with their prayers and tears, and heartily recommend them to the conduct and grace of God; beseeching him that he would take them under his own immediate care and tuition. The story of the pious and devout Monica, the mother of St. Augustine, is well known. That singularly good woman had used her utmost efforts to engage her son in a holy and Christian life; yet all seemed to be to no purpose; he continued in his extravagancies, and would not listen to her pious remonstrances: however, she did not give over caring for his soul; for, when her exhortations and advices could not any more reach him, she had recourse unto her prayers and tears, which was the reason that a good Bishop told her for her comfort, that it could not be, that a son, for whom she had shed so many tears, should perish. This accordingly came to pass; her labours were rewarded, and her prayers answered, and she had the pleasure to see the son of her tears a son of devotion and eminent sanctity. An example this is which affords the overseers of youth both an excellent pattern for imitation, and a good ground of encouragement for continuing their endeavours, even when there is little appearance of success.

With respect to these disappointments complained of, it ought to be seriously considered, whether some important flaw or other in their manner and conduct, may not have been the cause. Perhaps they have not in their instructions urged the necessary and essential truths and duties of Christianity, but laid the stress of religion on things that will not bear it; or it may be, their endeavours have been faint and remiss and interrupted, not pursued with vigour and constancy, not managed with seriousness; or peradventure their conversation has not been exact and regular; and so, though they have given the youth good precepts, yet they have set before them a bad example; or, in a word, they may not have had in any measure the qualifications I lately mentioned. Now, in all these cases we need not be surprised that the concerns of a pious education do not prosperously advance, or that the youth being under such a conduct as this, grow not in goodness and solid piety. Nothing can justly be expected from a management of this nature, but disappointments and degeneracy.

CHAPTER IX.

Objections to early Instructions in Religion.

THAT serious matters should be let alone till the follies and fervour of youth are over; till they have attained to maturity of judgment, and are more disposed to listen to sober counsels.

To this I answer, that God hath otherwise determined: " Train up a child in the way he should go (saith divine wisdom), and when he is old he shall not depart from it."

Childhood and youth are vanity.—They are so indeed, when left undisciplined, and permitted to follow the swing of their corrupt inclinations and passions.

Others represent that many of the youth are froward, cross, and perverse in their tempers; that they reject and despise all good advice; that they cannot be kept under any discipline, but, in spite of all that can be done or said to them, will follow their own courses and their own wills; and, therefore, that it were folly, and but lost labour, to make any attempt on such stubborn and rebellious minds, there being no reasonaale prospect of doing them any good.

In answer to this, it must be owned, that the tempers of children are very different; some are mild and manageable, of sweet and agreeable dispositions, and ready to comply with the injunctions that are given them. Others again are of rough, wild, and untowardly natures, and such as the discouragement just now proposed describes them; but even of these I would say, how hard or improbable soever their cure and reformation, and the introducing a better temper into them may appear to be, yet it ought not to be entirely despaired of, nor given up as altogether impossible. A piece of ground, that is full of thistles and thorns, and overgrown with weeds, promises very little; and yet by culture and improvement, and the kindly influences of the heavens, in moderate rains and a cherishing warmth, may become fruitful and produce abundance of useful herbs and pleasant flowers: just so a youth that is of a froward temper, and hath many other bad qualities, by a prudent management, and diligent endeavours to acquaint him with the truths and powers of religion, may, with the blessing of God and the influence of his grace, be made docile, and become serious and devout: for these aids we must earnestly pray, and on them humbly depend.

CHAPTER X.

*Teachers and Parents earnestly requested to consider,
whether some bad or mistaken Conduct may not
have contributed, if not to beget, yet to heighten
and improve, this Perverseness of Temper they complain of.*

THERE are two extremes into which parents are
prone to run : some are so excessively fond of their
children, that they indulge them in all their appetites ; they cannot endure to put them upon any
thing that is ungrateful and uneasy to them, or to
cross their humours ; and rather than chastise them
when a just occasion offers, they will excuse their
crimes ; or, if they chance at any time to give them
a few blows or stripes, too often in a fit of passion,
they soon after hug the fondling, and by so doing
baffle the design of the chastisement. And pray,
what can be expected should be the consequence of
such a conduct as this, but that the children having
been from their very infancy allowed to follow their
own wills, without any effectual curb or check,
should, as they advance in years, still become more
and more headstrong? for, the habit of gratifying their
appetites at random, and pleasing their own humours
in every thing, being so very agreeable to corrupt
nature, and now by long custom rooted in them, will
make them impatient of discipline and government,

and ready to kick at whatever would oblige them to act contrary to their beloved inclination. Whereas, if parents had by proper methods begun early to break their self-will, and train them up to obedience and subjection, there would not, I suppose, be so much ground to complain of the perverseness of youth as there is at present.

Some parents, on the other hand, are too rigorous and severe. Their chastisements are fierce and passionate, and managed without regard to religion or natural affection, and without any consideration of the quality of the offence.

All faults, and even trivial ones, are punished with rigour. It is against this indiscreet severity, I doubt not, that St. Paul cautions, when, once and again, he enjoins parents not to provoke their children to wrath, lest they be discouraged. Certainly, such a barbarous treatment as this is, will beget in them an aversion to discipline and government, and render their parents and instructors frightful and unacceptable to them; so that they will think it a grievance to be in their company. Their presence is a terror to them, and the tasks they impose, uneasy and disagreeable. In short, it will either break and crush their spirits or turn them desperate; and when matters go thus, the youth, indeed, may become stubborn and rebellious; but then their parents and overseers are in a great measure to be blamed for it.

From all this it evidently appears, that the middle course between both these extremes, is that which should be followed. The authority of the instructors of youth ought to be paternal; that is, gentle and winning; yet, so as never to countenance and indulge them in any thing that is criminal, or allow them to contract vicious habits: on the contrary, when they see any tendencies towards these appear in them, they should awfully check and reprove them; and if these softer methods should not prove effectual to dislodge the appearances of corruption, they are indispensably obliged to make use of the rod of correction. But these very chastisements should be tempered with love and endearments: they should at these rencounters so behave themselves, that the children may be sensible that it is not humour or passion, but a real design to do them good, that forces them to these severer courses. Such a kind and obliging behaviour toward them, will extremely recommend both the persons and the authority of their teachers to them, and make them very tender of doing any thing that may offend.

One thing more I desire may be seriously considered on this head; and that is, that the first and great thing wherein this authority ought to be employed, is to train up children in the denial of their own wills, and to render them perfectly obedient and submissive, and to begin the attempt as early as possible. Certainly this is one of the greatest kindnesses that can be done them, and even to their instructors too; for, by their being thus accustomed to resign their wills to the conduct of others, they become mild and tractable; and so that perverseness and obstinacy of temper, so much complained of in many of the youth, would be happily prevented; there being no one thing that more effectually contributes to beget and cherish it, than an unrestrained liberty, for several years, to follow their own wills, and to please them in every thing.

There are, in fine, others that object, or rather complain, that though they use their best endeavours to bring up their children in Christian piety, yet all seems to no purpose; the reason is, because any good impressions they make upon the minds, are soon defaced by the example and conversation of those of their own age, whose education is not looked after.

The youth, they say, are generally very corrupt and vicious, and it is very hard for a child, who is naturally prone to imitate what he sees frequently acted before him, though otherwise carefully educated, to preserve this innocency in the company of wicked boys; so that unless either they could keep their children so close, as not to have any opportunities of correspondency or familiarity, which is not possible for those who live in cities and public places to do; or that the endeavours of a pious education were more universal; it is needless, they think, for a few to attempt any thing that way. To all this I have the following considerations to oppose.

It must, indeed, be acknowledged, that the ground of this complaint is but too true ; that is, that parents and others are generally negligent in looking after the spiritual concerns of children ; that the youth are for the most part very vicious, and that bad examples have a most infecting influence.

However, the inference that they pretend to draw, namely, that it were folly for a few to attempt the pious education of their children, is not just ; for, the negligence of others will not excuse yours ; you must do what you know to be your duty, and leave the issue to God. If others will not do theirs, they are accountable for it to the God of the spirits of all flesh : in the mean time you have the satisfaction, that your conscience bears you witness, that you have neither wholly omitted, nor performed remissly, what you were bound to do in this weighty and important duty.

The general corruption of the youth should be so far from discouraging, that it should rather awaken and excite your zeal and diligence to lessen the number, by rescuing as many as you can out of it, or at least to prevent its increase, by breeding up those you have charge of in the fear of God.

Who knows what the efforts of a few pious parents and schoolmasters may, by the blessing of God, produce ? May we not hope, that others

E

might be animated by their zeal and diligence; and especially when they observe, how prosperously those children that are under the conduct of religious and careful instructors, advance in Christian piety, and in favour with God and man?

CHAPTER XI.

Our unruly Passions the great Enemies of the divine Life.

To make a discovery of the enemies of the divine life, I would consider a little those great disturbers of the quiet and repose of our minds, those usurpers over our reason, those direful incendiaries which raise so many tumults and commotions, both in our own bosoms and all around us—I mean our turbulent and unruly passions. " The wisdom that is from above, is pure and peaceable, gentle and easy to be entreated, full of mercy and good fruits, without partiality and without hypocrisy." But a soul that is under the power and dominion of black and furious passions, is evidently the reverse of all this; it is stormy and contentious, fierce and froward, injurious and cruel, stubborn and inexorable, full of spite and rancour, animated by self-love, and guided by self-will. Such dispositions as these are directly opposite to those amiable graces which make up the essential characters of a true Christian; and the longer they are allowed to continue in the soul, the more indisposed and averse it becomes to entertain the motions of the spirit of love, sweetness, and benignity. It is by letting these fierce and untowardly passions have an uncontrolled sway, that the interests of corrupt nature get a full establishment in the soul, and that men are transformed into devils. And therefore it cannot but be the advantage as well as the duty of all, vigorously to endeavour to suppress them, both in themselves and in all for whose happiness they are interested.

And in order to this, let parents and instructors be careful, that they do not needlessly and too often irritate and exasperate the minds of children, and so awaken their passions; but endeavour, as much as possible, to preserve them in a smooth and gentle, easy and agreeable temper; for it is certain, that by their being always kept fretting and crying, they become habitually froward, stormy, and passionate; and when parental authority degenerates into tyranny and caprice, it will be so far from reforming what is wrong, that it will dispose their minds to disobedience and contempt, and cherish perverseness and ill-nature. But if in their own conversation, parents set before their children the example of meekness and gentleness, patience and contentment, love and forbearance, and such graces as are most opposite to the irascible passions; this would be a very powerful means of instilling the same dispositions into them, as children are naturally prone to imitate what they see the parents practise. As a further means of checking their passions, let children never be allowed to do any thing that may excite or gratify ill nature, hatred, or revenge. A celebrated writer says, " I have frequently observed in children, that when they have got possession of any poor creature, they are apt to use it ill. They often torment and treat very roughly young birds, butterflies, and other poor animals which fall into their hands, and that with a seeming kind of pleasure. This should be watched in them, and if they incline to any such cruelty, they should be taught the contrary usage. For the custom of tormenting and killing animals will by degrees harden their minds towards men; and they who delight in the sufferings and destruction of inferior creatures, will not be apt to be very compassionate or benign to those of their own kind. Children should from the first be taught, not to kill or destroy any living creature, unless it be for the preservation or advantage of some other that is nobler." Though the principle of this inhuman disposition be unquestionably rooted in our degenerate nature, yet if we consider it as a habit, it is certainly excited and kept alive by custom and conversation; for, as the same author adds, " People may teach children to strike, and laugh when they hurt, or see harm come to others. And they have the example of most about them to confirm them in it. All the entertainment and talk of history is principally of fighting and killing. And the honour and renown bestowed on conquerors, who for the most part are but the great butchers of mankind, further mislead young minds, who by this means are led to think slaughter the laudable business of life, and the most heroic virtue. This ought carefully to be watched, and early remedied, so as to settle and cherish the contrary temper of benignity and compassion in the room of it."

Let parents frequently remind their children, that if they will follow the impulse of their wrath and anger, malice, envy, and revenge, they will infallibly forfeit the repose and quiet of their own minds, and be consequently miserable. For, when these passions are allowed to rage and domineer without control, they necessarily create such storms in the mind, that, " like the troubled sea, it cannot rest."

Let young people be recommended often to think on those Scriptures that warn against the indulgence of such passions; such as the following: " Let all bitterness, and wrath, and anger, and clamour, and evil speaking, be put away from you." " Recompense to no man evil for evil."—" Avenge not yourselves; but rather give place unto wrath."— But particularly let them be directed to " look unto Jesus, the author and finisher of their faith, who endured the cross and despised the shame;" that is, underwent all the rude and barbarous treatment of an unthankful and unbelieving world, with admirable meekness and patience. For, when " he was reviled, he reviled not again; when he suffered, he threatened not."—" But as a sheep before her shearers is dumb, so he opened not his mouth." Doubtless, to consider the behaviour of Him who was innocence itself, when injured, reproached, and ill treated, cannot but powerfully engage us to conform to so lovely a pattern, and resolutely to study to be meek and patient under the most exasperating provocations. And in order to reduce these sentiments to practice, when children complain of the little injuries and affronts they have received from their companions, their parents must engage them to bear such treatment with meekness and patience, telling them they must suffer greater things than these for the love of Jesus: that if their Redeemer was so ill-treated in this wicked world, they should be content to share a little of the same usage, " since the servant is not above his Lord"—" that they must suffer with him if they would reign with him." Thus ought parents to mitigate and divert the resentments of their children, never suffering them spitefully to threaten, or take vengeance on the offenders, but rather oblige them readily to forgive those that have injured them, and do them some little civility or kindness, thereby teaching them to " overcome evil with good." It is true, when children deliberately and wilfully do some considerable hurt to their companions, then their parents or governors must not fail to chastise them; but still the injured must be taught not to rejoice, or take pleasure in the sufferings of the offender, but rather be grieved that his wicked nature prompted him to do such things as exposed him to punishment, and heartily wish that his chastisement may reform and amend him. Thus must parents early acquaint their children with the maxims of the cross of Jesus Christ, and lead them to practise accordingly. I know such parents as conform unto the world, and follow its dictates in educating their children, will say, that to train them up in this manner, would be to render them cowardly and pusillanimous, to inspire them with sneaking and sheepish dispositions: that for their part they are far better pleased to see their children bold and courageous, apt to contend with, and domineer over their playfellows, and take vengeance on those that offend them; that these are the indications of life and spirit. Thus do the world and corrupt nature dictate. But, alas! they are most grievously mistaken: for, true courage does not consist in a heat and ferment of the blood, but in obtaining that composure and submission of mind, that no mournful event can raise any violent commotions within us. He is the bravest hero that enters the field against himself, and combats his own unreasonable and stormy affections, and continues the contest till he get such dominion over them, that no temptations will prevail with him to be either envious in want, impatient in suffering, angry at contempt, or malicious and revengeful under injuries and provocations.

It will also be necessary to enjoin children to guard carefully against the first risings of passion; and as soon as they begin to appear, endeavour vigorously to divert them by some one or other of the considerations above mentioned; or, if they cannot at first wholly prevent their making a disturbance within, at least to hinder their breaking out in exasperating and opprobrious language, since, if once we give them this liberty, they can hardly afterwards be managed and restrained. Whence it is evidently our interest to crush these cockatrices in the egg, and quench our passions while they are yet but a spark.

CHAPTER XII.

Parents and Teachers urged to recommend the follow-
ing Considerations to their Children and the Youth
under their Care, to dissuade them from gratifying
their irascible Passions.

FIRST.

THAT if they follow the swing of their wrath and anger, envy and revenge, they will infallibly forfeit the repose and quiet of their own minds, and consequently be miserable in this world: for, when these passions are allowed to rage and domineer without control or restraint, they necessarily create storms in the mind, and make it like the troubled sea that cannot rest.

SECOND.

While in this world we must expect to be encompassed with continual crowds of evil accidents, some or other of which will be continually pressing upon or jostling against us; so that, if our minds are sore and uneasy, and over-apt to be affected with evil, we shall be continually pained and disquieted.

Men imagine, that by giving vent to their passions, they ease and allay the evils that befall them; yet, in effect they do but increase and aggravate them, because they add the torment of an outrageous anger to the indignities that are offered them; and the smart of peevish impatience to the sufferings that happen to them, and make *their* want more uneasy, through an invidious pining at *another*'s fulness; and sharpen the injuries they meet with, by a malicious and revengeful resentment of them.

THIRD.

Let it be gravely represented to them, that these passions, if they are indulged and continued in till they convert into inveterate habits, do necessarily sink the soul into the miseries of eternity: for, when a man goes into the other world with these black and ill-natured passions about him in their full vigour, and without ever having used any effectual endeavours to suppress and mortify them, he then carries his hell in his very bosom. What torment-ors will they prove when an extreme rage and hate, envy and revenge, shall be altogether like so many hungry vultures preying on our hearts; and our minds continually baited and worried with all the furious thoughts which these outrageous passions can suggest; when, with the meagre eye of envy, we shall look up towards the regions of happiness, and incessantly pine and grieve at the felicity of those that inhabit them; when, through a sense of our own follies, and the miserable effects of them, our rage and impatience shall be heightened and boiled up into a diabolical fury; and when at the same time an inveterate malice against all we converse with, and a fierce desire of revenging ourselves upon those who contributed to our ruin, shall, like a wolf in our breasts, be continually gnawing and feeding upon our souls: what an unsupportable hell shall we be to ourselves! Doubtless that outward hell to which bad spirits are condemned, is very terrible; but I cannot imagine but that the worst of their hell is within themselves,—for, wrath and envy, malice and revenge, are both the nature and the plague of devils. If, then, these rancorous affections have such a malignant influence as to blacken angels into devils, and make *them* the most miserable who were the most happy creatures, how can we ever expect to be happy, so long as we indulge and harbour them ?

FOURTH.

Let the young be led to mortify their irascible passions by exercising the opposite graces.

That they put on bowels of mercies, kindness, humbleness of mind, meekness, long suffering; that they forbear one another; and that, above all these things, they put on charity or love; which, if it be seated and prevails in the soul, will prove the most sovereign antidote against these black and unmanning passions: for, " charity suffereth long, and is kind; charity envieth not, charity vaunteth not itself, is not puffed up, doth not behave itself unseemly, seeketh not her own, is not easily provoked, thinketh no evil, rejoiceth not in iniquity, beareth all things, believeth all things, hopeth all things."

FIFTH.

But, above all, let it be recommended to them, earnestly to pray that the good Spirit of God, the Spirit of peace and love, would come and dwell in their souls, and, by his gracious presence and operations, sweeten, smooth, and calm their fierce, stormy, and rugged dispositions, and fill their hearts with his peaceful and quieting fruits. In order to the casting out these devilish passions, it is necessary that we use humble, frequent, and fervent prayers, and invoke a power greater than our own to our assistance, in order to crush and dislodge these furies that our corrupted natures have produced.

A Youth at Prayer to his heavenly Father, for Strength and Grace to overcome the Violence of his Passions.

O my God and my Father! I come humbly to implore thy gracious aid to relieve me. Alas! I feel many disorderly and turbulent passions rising within me, that make me like the troubled sea, that put me in a ferment, and that ruffle and interrupt the quiet and serenity of my mind. I feel the boilings of proud anger, the resentment of bitter revenge, and the workings of pale envy, which not only discover themselves in my face by unbecoming looks, but also burst out at my tongue in opprobrious reviling language, unsuitable to my holy profession: so that the heavenly spark which thou hast kindled in my bosom is in danger of being smothered and overwhelmed by the fierce and rude attacks of my outrageous passions. O Lord, I am ashamed and blush, that I who have been consecrated to be a follower of the meek and lowly Jesus, should have any disposition, or betray any thing in word, that were unworthy of, unlike to my blessed Master: Alas! that I have not more effectually learned these sweet and endearing lessons of goodness and gentleness, of meekness and patience, of charity and good will, that he has taught me both by example and precept.

My dearest Lord, grant that I may have thee always before my eyes, and labour through thy grace, to imitate thy lovely carriage and behaviour under provocations and injurious treatment. O breathe into my soul thy spirit of kindness and charity, of tranquillity and peace; and extinguish in me all corrupt and rancorous passions, and whatever is inconsistent with thy life in me. May my anger be turned against what dishonours and displeases thee, my hatred against sin and vice, and my revenge exercised upon my old man and his deceitful lusts.

And finally, O merciful Saviour, grant me the grace to keep my heart with all diligence, and so carefully to watch the motions of my inward man, that when any temptation comes in my way which may awaken my passions, I may resist its force and suppress them in their first appearance, and, in humble dependence on thy mighty aid, continue wrestling with them and controlling them, till at last, through thy grace, I have gained thee; and to thee shall be all the glory for ever and ever. Amen.

CHAPTER XIII.

Answer to the Objection, that the Life of a Christian is sad and melancholy.

SOME persons may insinuate from what I have stated, that the life of a Christian must be very melancholy and pensive, wholly made up of bitter ingredients, and deprived of all pleasure and solace, and consequently that the whole is calculated rather to frighten some, than to engage and invite to the practice of piety. True it is nevertheless, that Christ's *yoke is easy*, and *his burden light;* for truth itself hath asserted it. But to whom is it so? To the *true* disciple, to him that cometh to this Divine Master, enters his school, learns of him, and takes up his yoke with cheerfulness and by choice, because it is his, and will lead to his rest, to his sweet presence, and to the enjoyment of him; that is, to a soul animated by love, as every sincere disciple is. Now, no task is grievous to him that loves. Love can turn labour, toil, and pains, into sweetness and delight. The commands of a beloved, especially a beloved so infinitely recommended as the Lord Jesus is, cannot be painful. Every thing he enjoins is pleasing and agreeable, whatever difficulties may otherwise be in it; every burden that he imposes, is not only tolerable but grateful; for love bears up the weight, and sweetens the fatigue. To such a disciple even those exercises of the Christian life which seem most afflicting, such as self-denial, bearing the cross, contrition, sacrificing the old man, and the like, have pleasure inseparably annexed to them, which the holy Scriptures, and the experience of the saints, abundantly testify. However, this does not say, but flesh and blood, and corruption, may murmur at what restrains and bears hard upon them, as certainly the yoke of Christ does; and therefore that which is here said to be an *easy* yoke, and a *light* burden, is elsewhere, and with respect to the old man and his lusts, called a strait gate, and a narrow way; so that it is plain, the holy Jesus never gave any commandment, never made any promise, never uttered any doctrine, that does in the least favour sin.—No, he came into the world with design to make an end of it, to destroy the works of the devil, and to " bring in everlasting righteousness."

I trust the serious consideration of the above may serve to evince, that the native tendencies of our holy religion are to remove the *true* causes of melancholy, to introduce a solid peace and serenity into our minds, and to prevent those black and despairing apprehensions, those direful agonies and convulsions of soul, that will in the end be the necessary consequences of a dissolute and irreligious life.

CHAPTER XIV.

The Happiness of early Piety.

HAPPY, thrice happy are they, who are prevailed upon to enter betimes on the ways of religion, who consecrate the choicest portions, the prime and vigour of their years, to the service of their God, and engage in the imitation of their Redeemer, before the corruption of nature is heightened by vicious habits, and a custom of sinning has rendered them insensible to the voice and calls of God, and hardened them into a wretched unconcern for their souls. Alas! that the mean and sordid pleasures of sin, the poor and contemptible enjoyments of flesh and sense, or the momentary vanities of this world, should so far infatuate the minds of youth, as to make them disregard those things which would improve their natures, ennoble their faculties, refine their dispositions, raise them up unto the life of God, and qualify them for his presence and glory! O how great is the loss that these sustain! how solid are the joys, how sweet the peace, how glorious the privileges, which they forfeit! and how certain as well as deplorable are the miseries in which those involve themselves, who in their younger years prefer a sensual to the divine life! O that all such as have the charge of these future hopes of church and state, yea and of heaven too, their parents and teachers, their tutors and governors,

would begin early to employ their utmost care and
skill in exposing the folly and madness of vice and
irreligion, in setting before them the beauties of that
blessed life I have been describing, and in persuading
them to enter the paths that lead to it. Alas! of
how little value are all the other offices of kindness they may do for them, if this one thing, this
great and necessary thing, be neglected or carelessly
managed! What are all those pursuits which they
endeavour with so much cost of time and pains, to
improve them in, but trifles and impertinencies, in
comparison of this? What are the riches and trea-
sures of this earth, when compared with the un-
searchable riches of Christ? What is the learning,
the wisdom and philosophy, the arts and sciences of
the world, when put in the balance with that wisdom that maketh wise unto salvation? What are
all the manners, and fashions, and dresses, which
are taught with so much exactness, studied with
so much pains, and imitated with such nicety?
What are all these vanities, I say, in comparison
with those manners and those dresses which fit and
qualify for eternal life? I mean the Christian graces
and virtues, those ornaments and that attire, on
which God sets so high a value. Ah! what account
can those overseers of youth give of themselves to
the Father of spirits, who study to improve such of
his offspring as are committed to their trust, only in
those things that regard time, but use no serious
diligence to instruct them in the principles of piety,
to guide them into the new life, and to prepare them
for a happy eternity! For, after all their pains and

labour, a youth that is vicious and profane, however learned he may be in human arts and sciences, makes but a mean figure in the eyes of God and good men. And a young lady, however exquisitely she may be accomplished in every thing that can recommend her to the world; yet if she is unadorned in her mind, if she is without purity and devotion, modesty and virtue, she is but a contemptible being, and unworthy of any regard. So that those teachers and governors of youth, who neglect the culture of their nobler parts, and the concerns of their salvation, whatever they may hope for from men, for being instrumental in accomplishing their children after the way of the world, they can have no comfortable prospect of being rewarded by God.

CHAPTER XV.

*Prayer for a Youth who feels his Need of being
created anew in Christ Jesus.*

O MOST holy Majesty, thy hands have made and
fashioned me; but now, alas! I am a poor degenerate creature; I feel in my whole man the deplorable
effects and consequences of sin; it hath lamentably
disordered and defiled all the faculties and power of
both soul and body. But, O my God, though sad experience has taught me a great deal of that corruption that is in my nature, I pray, that thy heavenly
light may discover it to me more and more, and
make me so to know it, as that I may truly hate it,
and penitently bewail it. I feel in myself, not only an
inability, but a backwardness, to do that which is
good and well-pleasing in thy sight. There is a law
in my members that warreth against the law of
my mind, and which, alas! too often prevails over
me. But, adored be thy great name, who hast re-
lieved me against this distress, in that thou hast
given me assurance of divine aid, and that thy grace
will prevent and assist my endeavours, will begin,
advance, and perfect my salvation, and work in me
both to will and to do.

I see, O Lord, how absolutely necessary this
precious grace is for me; for, without it, I can do
nothing: and it is only by its mighty operations,

that purity and beauty, life and vigour, health and soundness, can be restored to my soul. When any serious thoughts, any pious motions, any purposes, arise in my heart, I can impute it to no other cause but thy gracious inspirations. O grant that I may desire them with ardour and importunity. Communicate unto me, I beseech thee, these living waters, which thou hast promised to give, and to give liberally, unto them that ask thee. Thou art not wont to send the longing soul away empty from the fountain of life. Thy merciful ears are open to the cries of the afflicted and destitute, that invoke thee with fervour and seriousness, and thou graciously answerest their expectations by seasonably and plentifully supplying their wants. Lord, I hope I thirst after these precious influences, whereby my inward man may be renewed, may blossom as the rose, grow up as the lily, revive as the corn, and flourish as the palm-tree, and be united to the living Vine. Amen.

CHAPTER XVI.

Prayer for a Youth who is seeking the Wisdom from above.

O THOU great and adorable Teacher, the Teacher of the inward man, and the fountain of true wisdom, vouchsafe, I beseech thee, to take me betimes under thine own conduct, and to begin early to instruct me in the saving knowledge of thee, and of thy dear Son, whom to know is life eternal! O eternal Truth! teach thou me by thyself! Men can only reach my ears, but thou canst touch my heart. Their care may imprint thy laws on my memory, but thou canst put them in my inward parts, and turn them into living principles of obedience and a holy life. It is only under the influence of thy divine instruction, that I can advance successfuly in true religion, and attain to solid virtue. The words that thou speakest, they are spirit and they are life. Thy teaching is accompanied with efficacy and power; it enlightens the mind, purifies the heart, and in the hidden part it will make me to know wisdom. O my heavenly Father! give me those good things which thou bestowest on thy children that ask them of thee. Fill me with the fruits of thy Spirit, those lovely ornaments which thou so highly prizest, and whereby I shall be made conformable unto the image of thy Son. O suffer me not to take up with a form of godliness, with the outward shows and appearances of it which can only recommend me to men; but, since thou art the God of the heart, and desirest truth in the inward parts, grant, I pray thee, that it may be my daily care to have it vitally seated in my soul, to possess it really, and to feel its divine power prevailing over all that is vicious and corrupt in me, and animating me to all sorts of holy practices; that so all my religious performances may be as so many vital actions proceeding from a living principle and root; to the glory of thy name, through Jesus Christ my Lord. Amen.

PART THE SECOND.

BIBLE LECTURES

FOR

YOUTH.

RELATION OF GOD AS A FATHER.

" Our Father."

THE relation of a father is sweet and endearing; but how infinitely are the advantages and endearments increased, when the blessed God owns it, whose love, and fulness, and power, are equally infinite. Thus he stands related to all sincere Christians; and that not in a larger sense only, as they are his creatures, but in a stricter and more comfortable sense, as they are born of him, partake of his nature, bear his image, and represent him in their disposition and practice, and behave themselves as his dutiful and obedient children. Hence our Saviour, in his discourses to his disciples, so often recommends God to them under the lovely designation of their heavenly Father; and enjoins them and all his faithful followers, to eye him in their prayers, under this aspect; "When ye pray, say, Our Father." And what may not the children of such a Father expect? He graciously assures them, that all those vast and comfortable privileges which the relation of a Father involves, shall be bestowed on them; such as tenderness and compassion; " Like as a father pitieth his children, so the Lord pitieth them that fear him."

Instruction: " What man is he that feareth the Lord? him shall he teach in the way that he shall choose." Seasonable correction: " Whom the Lord loveth, he correcteth, even as a father the son in whom he delighteth." Provision: " Take no care, saying, What shall we eat, or what shall we drink, or wherewithal shall we be clothed? for your heavenly Father knoweth that you have need of all these things." Protection: " The eye of the Lord is upon them that fear him, to deliver their soul from death."

And all these advantages are of such a nature, and given in such a way, as is worthy of the Father of mercies. Compassion that never fails; not merely an affectionate and ineffectual sympathy (such as often the compassions of the most tender earthly parents are), but relieving and consolatory instructions, which give not the speculative notions only, but the reality and sweetness of divine things; corrections that do not really hurt or grieve, but reclaim, amend, and purify. Provisions, whereby not only the body is furnished with what it stands in need of, but which answer the necessities of the soul, and satisfy all its capacities. A protection, which not only prevents and averts dangers and troubles, but also prepares the soul for them, disposes it to welcome them, and endure them with patience; which powerfully supports under them, and graciously delivers from them. O! how unspeakable a privilege is it, to be the children of such a Father! What wonder that St. John, when viewing it, and discoursing on it, exclaims in a rapture, " Behold what manner of love the Father hath bestowed on us, that we should be called the children of God."

THE FIRST GREAT COMMANDMENT: THE LOVE OF GOD.

MATT. XXII. 37.

Thou shalt love the Lord thy God with all thy heart, and with all thy soul.

ALL the advantages that the Gospel furnishes us with, ought to be made use of, in order to engage the young heart to aspire with all its ardency after the love of God, and of all his creatures in him, and for his sake. This is the great design of all religion, as that wherein all the other duties centre and terminate; and that which is the very soul, and life, and beauty of them, which puts a value on them, and without which they cannot be acceptable.

Under the blessed Gospel, the great precept of love to God and man, is reinforced with a great many new endearments and motives; such as the surprising manifestation of the love and good will of God, in the redemption of the world; the condescensions and sufferings, the melting charity and compassions of the Son of God; the graces, assistances, and consolations of the Holy Spirit; the publication of pardon and reconciliation, and the evident promises of eternal life; all which, when seriously considered, ought inviolably to oblige us both to make all the returns of love to God, that are possible for us, and to imitate in our carriage towards men, the methods of mercifulness and condescension of the Gospel towards us.

THE GOSPEL INVITATION.

—

MATT. XI.

Come unto me, all ye that labour and are heavy laden, and I will give you rest. Take my yoke upon you, and learn of me; for I am meek and lowly in heart; and ye shall find rest unto your souls: for my yoke is easy, and my burden is light.

THIS is the sum and substance of the Gospel call. Here our blessed Redeemer doth, with a great deal of tenderness and affection, invite all that labour and are heavy laden, that is, such as toil and disquiet themselves in vain and laborious pursuits, after satisfaction in created things and pleasures,— such as are burdened with uneasy and vexing cares— such as penitently groan under the sense and weight of the guilt and power and impurities of sin, and vehemently long for deliverance; such, I say, the holy Jesus invites to come unto him, that is, to enter into his school, to become his disciples, to resign themselves to his conduct and instruction, to submit to his cure, to depend on his grace and merits; and, in a word, to demean themselves suitably to all those relations he bears to them as their Redeemer. And all that are in these dispositions he assures that he will give them rest; that is, he will satisfy their desires, solace their sorrows, relieve them of their burdens, heal their distempers, cleanse them from the defilements of sin, deliver them from their slavery, procure and apply their pardon, and finally advance them to a state of endless and perfect happiness; this is the marrow and substance of the great promises of the Gospel.

As to the terms, they are figuratively and more generally expressed by the phrase of coming unto him; but we have them more distinctly and more particularly set down in these words, " Take my yoke upon you, and learn of me;" that is, obey my precepts, and set me before you as your pattern; transcribe the divine virtues I exemplify unto you; and especially conform to me in the graces of humility and meekness, on which I put so dear a value, and whereof I give you a lively and continual copy in all my example.

Our Lord calls his commandments a yoke, because they check and restrain our corrupt inclinations, and oblige us to make constant and persevering resistances unto them; as also to endeavour to attain those gracious dispositions, which suppose and require the expulsion and crucifixion of the vicious habits and tendencies of our degenerate natures. But then he tells us, the tasks which he prescribes his disciples are light and easy. Certainly, they are so to those who are invigorated by the love of Jesus, and assisted by his grace, and such all his faithful followers are; for, though the precepts and counsels, if they be hard and severe sayings to flesh and blood, because they urge the extermination and death of the old man, yet this love of Jesus will render all the uneasinesses that appear in them easy, and its burdens light.

LUKE, IX. 23.

If any man will come after me, let him deny himself,
and take up his cross daily, and follow me.

THESE are the memorable words of the blessed
Jesus, wherein he declares what the terms are, which
all that would become his followers, and inherit the
glorious privileges that he hath merited for them,
must resolve to accept of, and to which they must
conform.

Our blessed Lord considered them as containing
one of the most essential maxims of the Gospel:
and, indeed, it is not possible to give a more just,
a more genuine, and a more perfect idea of a Christian, than that which is given to us in this passage:
" If any man will come after me;" that is, whoever
will own me as his Master and Teacher, and become
my disciple, I shall acquaint him beforehand with
what he must indispensably resolve to do. The first
and great lesson I set before him, and which he
must effectually learn and practise, is this: let him
deny himself; that is, he must renounce and despise,
forsake and hate all that is vicious and depraved in
him, though never so dear and valuable in his
eyes; all the lusts and passions, the appetites and
inclinations of the old man; all that issue from his
own corrupted heart, polluted and impure, darkened

and weakened, ignorant and foolish, the corrupt source of all evil.

Let him deny himself; that is, he must renounce and despise, forsake and hate all that is vicious and depraved in him, though never so dear and valuable in his eyes—all the lusts and passions, the appetites and inclinations of his old man—all his own wisdom and strength, and all the false appearances of religion, righteousness, and virtue, that are merely the product of his own lapsed faculties, and actually without the intervention of the operations of divine grace; in a word, all that naturally issues from his own heart, and merits no other treatment than crucifixion and death.

He must take up his cross daily; that is, resolutely and cheerfully embrace all those means that can contribute to root out and destroy our vicious and depraved inclinations, kill and crucify the flesh, with all its affections and lusts—those internal and daily strugglings which we have with our corruptions, those continual resistances and oppositions that we must make against attempts and efforts of the old man—those resolute controllings of the first appearance of our passions, and those generous refusals to comply with the vicious cravings of our inordinate appetites—those vigorous and stubborn endeavours to break the forces, and to turn the tide and current of our inveterate habits: those constant watchings, in order to discover the temptations of Satan, to defeat his artifices, and reject his insinuations. They err, and that very greatly, who imagine that there is no other cross but worldly tribulation, being ignorant that internal sorrow and the mortification of the flesh constitute the true cross, which, after the example of Christ, we are obliged daily to bear.

And follow me; that is, he must set me before him as his pattern, and conform to the copy that I have given him. Trace my footsteps, and walk as I walked—be content to meet with the same treatment from the world that I met with from it—suffer as I have done—be animated and influenced by the same spirit—practise the same virtues that I did—have the same gracious dispositions and inclinations that I had, while I tabernacled in mortal flesh.

Do not these words contain the marrow and fatness of Gospel morality? and as they are among the first lessons that were taught by our Lord and Maker, ought not youth to be made early acquainted with them?

CHRIST WEEPING OVER THE SINS AND MISERIES OF MEN.

" O Jerusalem, Jerusalem!"

HERE is a noble copy set before us, and most worthy of imitation. With what eagerness should the followers of the holy Jesus endeavour to transcribe it! How can they look on that, either in themselves or others, with unconcerned hearts and dry eyes, which drew sighs and tears from the Son of God? How sensibly was this great lover of souls touched, when he saw men taking courses that would infallibly ruin them! We are told by St. Mark, that " he was grieved because of the hardness of the hearts" of those among whom he had preached so many admirable sermons, and done so many glorious miracles, with design to convince and reclaim them. It pierced him with a deep sorrow to see that his gracious and charitable endeavours to do them good were rendered ineffectual by their wilful unbelief. How surpassing must that grief have heen, which attended these mournful accents of his over the rebellious obstinacy of Jerusalem: " O Jerusalem, Jerusalem, thou that killest the prophets and stonest them which are sent unto thee; how often would I have gathered thy children together, even as a hen gathereth her chickens under her wings, but ye would not." And moreover, his in-

comparable zeal for God greatly added to his sorrow
on these occasions; for how could it but vehemently
afflict his heart, to see that Sovereign Majesty whom
he so dearly loved, and to whom he knew all adoration, respect, and obedience were due, dishonoured
and blasphemed; to see his Spirit resisted, his offers
slighted, and all the methods of his love and grace
disregarded! Ah! it is a sad sign, that the " same
mind is not in us that was in Christ," when we can
see sin committed, and not bewail it; and God dis
honoured, without being troubled at it. Alas! should
we laugh at that which our Redeemer mourned for?
should that be matter of sport and mirth to us,
which put him to grief and tears?

The blessed Jesus, as he bewailed the sins of men,
so did he also the sad consequences of them. His
charitable heart was afflicted with the calamities
in which mankind had involved themselves, by
their apostasy from God. He was by a wonderful
sympathy so touched with their maladies as if they
had been his own; hence it is that St. Matthew af-
firms, that in his miraculously healing the diseased
with so much pity and tenderness, these words of
the prophet Isaiah were fulfilled, " Himself took our
infirmities, and bore our sicknesses." For, though
this prophecy was principally accomplished in Christ's
sufferings on the cross, where " he bore our sins in
his own body," yet the Evangelist assures us, that
it received a completion in his healing the sick, and
bearing their corporeal infirmities, by an admirable
compassion, which gave him so deep a sense of the

uneasiness and incommodities of their several distempers as if himself had been actually affected with them. Indeed it is hard to tell, how far a sincere and sympathizing charity may go in feeling the miseries of others. Daily experience shows how far even natural affection carries us in sharing the distresses of a dear friend or relation; how their pains and agonies, their groans and tears, almost transform us into fellow-sufferers with them. What shall we say then of the noble and undisguised, the vast and comprehensive charity of the Son of God! How deeply must it have made him share in the calamities of poor mortals! How tenderly doth he lament, not the sins only, but also the approaching desolations of Jerusalem! "When he beheld the city, he wept over it." He foresaw its future ruin and miseries in all their most aggravating and grievous circumstances, and shed tears with as lively a concern as if he had been actually a spectator of, or a partaker in, the calamities of that doleful tragedy. How feelingly did his bowels yearn over the poor widow of Nain, bewailing the death of her only son! "When he saw her he had compassion on her, and said unto her, Weep not." What emphatical discoveries of his sympathizing grief and tears did he give on meeting with the mourning sister and friends of Lazarus! "When Jesus saw Mary weeping, and the Jews also weeping that came with her, he groaned in his spirit, and was troubled." —"Jesus wept." The Gospel abounds with instances of these very tender and generous sympathies whereby our blessed Redeemer became a

4

fellow-patient with the miserable in all their afflictions. Here also the holy Jesus sets his followers a lovely pattern, to which he requires their conformity. He would have them do as the compassionate Samaritan, who when he saw in his way as he journeyed, a man stript naked, wounded, and left for half dead, had compassion on him, bound up his wounds, and poured oil into them, and took care of his full recovery. How diligently, therefore, should they endeavour to imitate his sweet and sympathizing temper, and share in the calamities of others, by a kind and charitable fellow-feeling! Nor let us forget, that as our Lord, when he bewailed the sins of men, laboured to convert the sinners, and in sympathizing with their miseries took care to remove them; so also ought his followers, as far as they are able, to endeavour to do. They must in their different capacities and stations, by their good examples, fervent prayers, kind admonitions, seasonable and discreetly managed reproofs, endeavour to reclaim from the sins they mourn for. They must, by all the methods that love will suggest, and their power can reach, contribute to relieve from the calamities they see others afflicted with. Tenderness, compassion, and bowels of mercies, constitute a considerable part of the image of the Son of God, are the fruits of his spirit, and the characters of his religion. Hence St. Paul exhorts us " to bear one another's burdens, and so fulfil the law of Christ;" —" to weep with them that weep;" and to " remember them that are in bonds, as bound with them."

CHRIST OUR PATTERN IN CONFLICT.

" I have overcome the world."

BEHOLD the Captain of our salvation! See how
he hath combated and defeated all our enemies!
Shall we content ourselves to be spectators only of
his courage and conflicts, and not imitators also?
Dare we own ourselves to be his followers, and yet
not accompany him into the field of battle? Can
we obtain the crown without a combat? No! hear
how himself determines the case: " To him that
overcometh, will I grant to sit down with me on
my throne, even as I also overcame, and am set
down with my Father on his throne." See here the
pattern both of our duty and our reward, and how
the former is the only way to the latter. Christ
overcoming is the pattern of our duty, and Christ
sitting on the throne, the pattern of our reward;
for it is a fixed and unalterable decree, that none
shall be crowned without being victorious, and that
we may conquer, we must wrestle and strive. And
to engage and encourage us to do this, our adorable
Redeemer did vouchsafe to become like one of the
sons of fallen Adam, and so put himself in a con-
dition of being attacked by our enemies, and accordingly came into the field of battle, sustained
their assaults, and put them to flight, and by so
doing he hath informed us whom we are to look on
as our enemies, that we might never afterwards
mistake them for friends. He hath acquainted us

with the weapons of our warfare, and taught the methods of managing them successfully; he hath let us see what mighty strength and assistance will be afforded us in combating; and not only convinced us of the possibility, but also given assurance of victory, if we continue under his conduct, and imitate the pattern he has set before us. And what should now hinder us from engaging immediately in this warfare? Are not all just grounds of fear and discouragement taken out of the way? Do not we know our enemies? Then why should we live any more in friendship with them? Are we not furnished with excellent weapons, and assurances of powerful aids? Where then is the pretence of weakness? Our Lord will not send us on a warfare in our own strength; his almighty Spirit and grace will accompany us to the field, and assist and direct us in the conflict; his holy angels will be our attendants and guardians, as soon as we enlist ourselves under his banners, so that " more and mightier are they that be with us, than they that be against us; greater is He that is in us, than he that is in the world;" and therefore we may be confident of victory, if we do not shamefully desert to the enemy, and thereby forfeit all our advantages, and return to the state of servitude and bondage. Is it not moreover by conflicts and wrestling that we must enter upon a state of triumph and glory? Is it not thus that the " kingdom of heaven suffereth violence, and that the violent take it by force?" Must we not " strive to enter in at the strait gate that leadeth unto life?" Or has our

Lord, in conflicting with our adversaries, so defeated them, as that we have no more need or occasion for resistance or opposition? No, by no means; for, as long as we continue in this world, we are in the field of battle, and our enemies are around us, yea even within us, and will not fail to attack us on all hands, and therefore we are still obliged to make opposition to them, unless we resolve tamely to be their slaves, and thereby inherit eternal misery. Our Redeemer indeed hath so vanquished the adversaries of our souls, that all who heartily become his disciples, resign themselves to his guidance, depend upon his power, follow his example, and persevere in a faithful adherence to him, shall through his grace infallibly become more than conquerors. But then still it is the character of a true follower of Jesus to be a combatant. And hence it is that we are so often enjoined, " so to run as that we may obtain; to endure hardship as good soldiers of Christ; to fight the good fight of faith; to resist the devil; to mortify the deeds of the body; and not to love, nor have friendship with the world." So that whoever doth not profess, in this state of trial and temptations, to be a soldier and combatant, and perseveres not in a resolute and vigorous opposition to the world, the devil, and the flesh, forfeits both his pretences to be a follower of Jesus, and his hopes of the glorious rewards of the other world, which are only promised to such as overcome. Has not the state of all the saints in this world, been one of struggling and conflicts? " We wrestle not," saith St. Paul, " against flesh and blood, but against principalities and powers, against the rulers of the darkness of this world, against spiritual wickedness in high places." Did they ever pretend to share in the joyful triumphs of eternity on any other terms but those of wrestling and conquering, after the example, and through the grace and power, of Jesus Christ? " I have fought a good fight,—henceforth there is laid up for me a crown of righteousness," was the Apostle's triumphant song in the view of his approaching change. With what face then can we pretend to expect that we shall be admitted to the fellowship of the saints in their triumphant state, who would not unite with them, nor follow their example when they were militant? we who have ever lived in profound peace with the enemies of our souls, who have been willing slaves to the devil, loved the world, and the things that are in the world, and gratified, and " made provision for the flesh to fulfil the lusts thereof;" we who either not at all, or but very faintly, have made any opposition to them, and soon returned again to amity and friendship with them?

Up then, and let us shake off our sloth and cowardice, let us resolutely turn our faces against these enemies, and never more enter into league or friendship with them; let us not dread their power, and cunning, and multitude, nor doubt but we shall at last overcome them; " for the Lord of Hosts is with us, the God of Jacob is our refuge."

THE LOVE OF JESUS.

" For the love of Christ constraineth us."

O MY soul, here is an object proper to entertain thy thoughts. It is the love of thy Redeemer! that love which is the source and spring of all thy blessings, that kind and benign force that engaged the Son of God to come and visit thee in the likeness of sinful flesh; to visit thee when thou hadst nothing that could have invited him; when, with the rest of the lapsed posterity of Adam, thou wast an enemy and a rebel, diseased in thy nature, and disaffected to thy cure. But this almighty and victorious love conquered all difficulties, answered all objections, surmounted all impediments, to fix on the children of men as its peculiar objects, though without any lovely qualities that might endear them, or merits to recommend them. O gracious and undeserved love! How can I, O blessed Saviour, be without love to thee, when I know that thou hast so deeply loved me? Shall the publicans and sinners outdo me in grateful returns? for even they love those that love them; and shall I be cold and indifferent towards thee, without devotion to thee, and desires after thee? How deservedly ought I to be anathema, if I love not the Lord Jesus Christ!

O blessed Jesus, why is my love in so dying a state? why doth not divine love exert its mighty efficacy in my heart? Is it because other loves and objects have seized it, and so filled my heart that there is no room left for thy love to enter? O my strength and my Redeemer, interpose, I beseech thee, the exceeding greatness of the power of thy grace, disunite my desires from self and creatures, purify and cleanse my soul, and let some sparks of thy pure and almighty love fall upon it, that may beget in it pious ardours and a heavenly warmth. O continue, I humbly entreat thee, to empty my heart of all impure loves, of all earthly affections, of all inordinate propensities towards created things and pleasures, till it become a habitation meet for thy love.

THE LOVE OF JESUS GRATEFULLY ACKNOWLEDGED

IN PURIFYING OUR SOULS FROM SIN.

O MERCIFUL Redeemer! when sin had for ever shut the doors of Paradise, and we had contracted dispositions inconsistent with pure and heavenly enjoyments, thou didst compassionately interpose, and by all that thou hast done and suffered for us, hast procured the opening of the kingdom of heaven to all believers. And now for thy sake we are kindly invited to return.

The blessed errand, O merciful Saviour, which brought thee down from the bosom of thy Father, was to seek and to save that which was lost, to rescue from the bondage of corruption, and to restore unto us the bliss and glory which we had sinned away: and because we could not repossess the undefiled inheritance until we were made meet for it, therefore thou camest to make an end of sin, and to bring in everlasting righteousness; to destroy the works of the devil in us, and to beautify our souls with heavenly graces; to redeem us from all iniquity, and to purify us for thyself as a peculiar people; and hast indispensably obliged all thy followers, not only to seek the heavenly kingdom, but also the righteousness which qualifies for it, by purifying themselves from all filthiness both of the flesh and spirit, and perfecting holiness in the fear of God. O forbid that I should give any countenance to sin in me, that I should indulge any corrupt lust, gratify any vicious inclination, or cherish any irregular appetites, knowing that without holiness no man shall see the Lord. O may it be my daily care through the Spirit to mortify the deeds of the body, to crucify my old man, to root out my wicked habits, to control my corrupt lusts, and strenuously to resist the importunities of my flesh and blood; that so endeavouring, in humble dependence on the influences of thy grace, to purify myself as thou art pure, I may at last become capable of being admitted into thy presence, and there to see thy glory, to be filled with thy joys, and to sing thy praises, world without end. Amen.

THE GREAT RULE OF MORALITY.

MATT. VII. 12.

*All things whatsoever ye would that men should do
unto you, do ye even so to them.*

Let us all remember, that, in order to practise this
maxim as we ought, the love of God must regulate
the exercise of it; for this is that noble principle
which directs to the most generous and purest measures in dealing with others. It is this that will
give us the truest and most genuine commentary on
this precept of our Redeemer, and teach us to observe it, both in the most extensive and in the most
excellent manner; whereas corrupt nature being a
blind and partial and selfish principle, will incline
either not to observe it at all, or dictate very falsely
or imperfectly concerning it.

The love of God illuminates the soul in which it
dwells, and inspires it with just and charitable inclinations; and as it knows the measures which the
Gospel prescribes in dealing by others, so it very
faithfully accommodates itself thereto. He that is
animated by divine charity, states himself in the con-
dition of others, and gives every body the same treatment that he would expect from them if he were
in their case. " He rejoices with them that rejoice,
and weeps with them that weep." Rom. xii. 15. He

remembers them that are in bonds as bound with them; and them that suffer adversity, as being themselves also in the body, and liable to the same calamities with others. He bewails the impenitent, reproves the sinner, instructs the ignorant, comforts the dejected, supports the weak, relieves the necessitous, visits the sick. He delivers the poor that crieth, and the fatherless, and him that hath none to help him. The blessing of such as are ready to perish comes upon him. He causes the widow's heart to sing for joy. He is eyes to the blind and feet to the lame. In a word—he endeavours as far as possible to have the same sense of the miseries of men that they have themselves, and ministers according to his ability the assistances that are proper to their respective conditions, as if the case were his own. And as he thus labours to feel and relieve the exigencies of the several cases of men; so, moreover, he views himself as clothed with the several relations in which others stand with respect to him, and carries it to them as dutifully, and bears their infirmities with as much tenderness and pity, as he could wish they should do to him, if he stood so related to them.

I PETER, III. 4.

The hidden man of the heart.

IT was this, as being the more valuable and nobler part of us, that the holy Jesus intended especially, and in the first place, to redress and reform, to rescue from the powers of darkness, and the impurities of vice, and to beautify and adorn with divine graces and accomplishments, and that in order to the full and perfect restoration of our whole man. It is here where he fixes his throne, and establishes his kingdom.

" The kingdom of God is within you:" and such also are the laws by which it is managed and governed; that is, they are internal and spiritual. If we take a view of the doctrines of our blessed Saviour, we shall quickly discover, that they all, and particularly the preceptive part of them, have a continual regard to the heart, and are calculated for the regulation of the motions of the inner man, and reach unto our most hidden and retired thoughts and inclinations. Not but our Lord hath also established laws concerning the outward man, for regulating its deportment; this he hath certainly done: but then laws are given to the outward man, as it is supposed to be in conjunction with and influenced by the inward, so that they are the motions and affections of the inward man that are regarded, when any thing is forbidden or commanded to the outward: and the performances and abstinences of the outward man, if separated from the correspondent and suitable motions in the inward, are of no value in the sight of God; for though, for instance, one should pray and praise vocally never so often—though he should read the holy Scriptures—though he should fast and give alms; yet, if he prays and praises without the inward devotion of the heart—if he reads without sincere resolution to obey—if he fasts without penitential contrition—and gives alms without charity and compassion; all this is of no account with the Searcher of hearts. Further, though one does not actually take away the life of his neighbour; though he abstain from grosser practices of uncleanness; yet, as long as he retains rancour and malice in his heart, and inwardly cherishes impure inclinations —his outward abstinences do not clear him from guilt; he is still, for all this, before God, reputed a murderer and unclean. Indeed, it is our outward man alone, that falls under the jurisdiction of the sovereigns of the world; and it is to it alone, that they can give laws, because it is only for the deportment of it, that they can call us to account; but it is the prerogative of the King of Saints to give laws to the hidden man of the heart, and he both can and will reckon with us for whatever is transacted there, though with never so much secrecy: because, " all things are naked and open unto the eyes of Him with whom we have to do ;" and as himself tells those of Thyatira, in his Epistle to them, " all the churches shall know, that it is He who searcheth the reins."

THE CHRISTIAN BEATITUDES.

THE Christian beatitudes I would have recommended to youth, as so many precious and invaluable jewels. O! what great and noble things are poverty of spirit, penitential mourning, meekness, an hungering and thirsting after righteousness, mercifulness, purity of heart, peaceableness, and a patient bearing of persecution for righteousness sake! These are sure and undeceiving characters of a true disciple of Jesus; these are both the ornaments that beautify and recommend, and the prime ingredients that constitute and form a sincere Christian. We may learn what value our Lord puts on them, from those precious and endearing promises which he hath annexed to each of them in particular. They surely cannot be mean and contemptible things, things of small moment and concern, that the holy Jesus so solemnly recommends, and puts on as a dress, that at once evinces both how necessary and how excellent they are! It is from these that we must judge of the goodness or badness of our state towards God and eternity; for it is certain, that proportionably as these graces are more or less, or not at all, discoverable in us—so accordingly we may safely conclude, that we are more or less, or not at all Christians. The marks which the blind and flattering self-love of men have set up are illusive; they satisfy us, that we are assured of heaven, though we want those dispositions that must qualify and prepare us for it. But the marks which truth itself hath established are certain and infallible, and cannot deceive us; they are those that we must search for in our hearts, in order to be assured of our title to the favour of God, and the glories of the heavenly world.

SOURCE OF THE DIVINE LIFE.

THE source of the divine life is from above, even from " Him with whom is the fountain of life," and whose prerogative it is to give life to the dead; and our Lord informs us, that it is He who communicates those living waters, which become in the soul " a well of water springing up into everlasting life." And here we may observe the great variety of expressions the Scriptures use concerning this holy principle. Sometimes it is represented by " God's dwelling in them;" by " Christ living in the heart ;" at other times, and very frequently, by " the law of the spirit of life in Christ Jesus," or the Holy Ghost inhabiting and influencing the inner man. And as all this clearly denotes the excellency of this life, and justly entitles it to the character of divine, so likewise it clearly points out the way by which we may be made partakers of it; namely, by addressing with frequency and fervour its adorable Author; who hath promised that " they that ask shall receive, they that seek shall find, and to them that knock it shall be opened." Let nothing then divert us from aspiring after a privilege so eminent and so glorious, and so indispensably necessary to us, as having God's good Spirit to be the blessed inhabitant of our souls. For, since our Lord has told us, that " our heavenly Father will give his holy Spirit to them that ask him;" and since this is the most essential and distinguishing mark of the true Christian (for, " if we have not the spirit of Christ, we are none of his"); we have every thing to encourage us to pray for it, because we are to address a Father— even our heavenly Father, whose tenderness and ability to do good, infinitely surpass those of any earthly father; and on the other hand, we have every thing to alarm us if we are without it; for, unless we are made "partakers of the Holy Ghost," we are only Christians in name and pretence, not in deed and truth— we can neither answer the dignity nor fulfil the obligations, and therefore can lay no just claim to the prize of the high calling of God in Christ Jesus.

The holy Spirit of God being the principle of the life of the regenerate, not only irradiates and enlightens their minds, whereby they become solidly acquainted with the things of God, but is also in their hearts a living source of love, joy, peace, long suffering, gentleness, goodness, faith, meekness, temperance, and of all sorts of divine virtues;—which are therefore called in holy Scripture the fruits of the Spirit. It is he that breathes into their souls those amiable and heavenly dispositions, whereby alone they can, on good grounds, be denominated meek and humble, patient, charitable, and ready to forgive, and which are the noblest endowments of the soul, and render it lovely and precious in the sight of God. The comeliness of pure minds is chiefly internal, seated in the heart, and in that respect obvious only to that all-penetrating eye, to which every thing is naked and open. But then it is very certain, that those holy dispositions which adorn the inward man will also beautify the life, and render the conversation such as becomes the Gospel, so that all who are familiar with these excellent ones, may observe in their shining examples the lovely images of the graces that animate their hearts. The regenerate do not live at random, and without regard to order; no, certainly: their actions are directed according to the most excellent maxims; for, as they " are born not of blood, nor of the will of the flesh, nor of the will of man, but of God;" so neither do they regulate their conduct according to the dictates of flesh and blood, and the corrupt wills of men, but according to the orders of the will of God. This good, wise, and perfect will, the will of their heavenly Father, is that which they endeavour always to have in their eye, and the injunctions which it gives are the compass by which they steer the course of their conversation. In a word, their hearts are enlarged, the light and love of God being shed abroad in them, and therefore they run the way of his commandments, which is to them a way of pleasantness, as well as paths of peace. Moreover, the Holy Spirit is the spirit of power and might, and they in whom he dwells, are " strong in the Lord," being " strengthened with might by his Spirit in the inner man;" and the significant emblem of a " well of water springing up," evidently imports that the divine life is no weak inefficacious thing, but that it continually exerts its vigour in some instance or other of piety and goodness. For such only as are animated by it, and consequently endued with power from on high, can bear up against the opposition of the world, withstand its insinuating temptations, control the importunities of flesh and blood, defeat the powers of darkness, and surmount all the difficulties they meet in the way to bliss, notwithstanding the fierce assaults that are made to oblige them to desert and abandon it.

DURABILITY OF THE DIVINE LIFE.

THE divine life is not a flash, nor a heat, that is soon over, no sudden paroxysms of devotion, no transient raptures which quickly vanish, and to which the motions of the animal and carnal life do within a little succeed. No; it is a stable and lasting thing, and renders those in whom it prevails, " steadfast, unmoveable, and always abounding in the work of the Lord." There are several persons, in whom one may observe some plausible appearances of a spiritual life; but the momentary duration of such appearances, and the speedy relapse of those in whom they are, into the gratifications of flesh, and blood, and corruption, plainly demonstrate, that they are shadowy and not real, false imitations only, and not genuine expressions of the new life. These are fluctuating and unstable souls; they take some promising steps in a religious course, but they soon weary and draw back; they shoot forth fair and high, but they quickly wither, and their goodly blossoms drop off: so that they do " not bring forth fruit to perfection, because they have no root in themselves." Whereas, those excellent ones, who are raised up into a divine life, are firm and steady, constant and unwavering; they cheerfully advance in the race that is set before them, and continue in it with patience. But it must be remembered, that I speak here of those, in whom this

blessed life is confirmed, and advanced into nature
and constitution; for, otherwise, it must be acknowledged, that this life in its infant state, is liable to
changes and vicissitudes, and may now and then
receive some wounds in its struggles and conflicts
with the life of the old man. But then, if they in
whom it is, in this state of weakness, will resume
their courage and their hopes, and believingly
recur unto, and depend upon the grace and Spirit of
Jesus Christ; He whose lovely character it is, that
he " will not break the bruised reed," but as the
good Shepherd, " will gather the lambs in his arm,
carry them in his bosom, and gently lead those
that are with young;" he, I say, will heal its
wounds, and reinforce it anew with his heavenly influences, so that it shall increase in strength, and at
last become victorious and triumphant.

GRADUAL PROGRESS OF THE DIVINE LIFE.

THERE is a great resemblance between the spiritual life and the natural; for, as the latter, from small beginnings, passes through several degrees of age and vigour, and at length arrives at perfection; so doth the former also: and hence the divine principle of it is compared to seed, which when sown in a proper soil, and cherished by the influences of heaven, springs up insensibly, and in process of time, according to its nature and kind, becomes a beautiful flower or a stately tree; by which similitude the gradual advances of the new life are very significantly represented to us. But, however, there is this remarkable difference, that the natural life, when it hath arrived at a certain period, begins to decline, its beauty decays, and its vigour abates; whereas, the spiritual life, to whatever period of age, or heights of perfection it may attain during the state of probation, is still capable of further improvements, and the longer it continues the stronger it becomes, and the more conspicuous are its excellent beauties. "The righteous," as the royal Psalmist by the Spirit of God informs us, "shall flourish like the palm-tree, and grow up as a cedar of Lebanon;" that is, they shall proceed from one degree of virtue and goodness to another, they shall abound yet more and more in light and love, and their graces become brighter and brighter. Nay, not only so, but, as the same inspired writer adds, " they shall bring forth fruit in old age;" for, though they wax old, yet the divine life in them continues blooming and verdant, and will put forth its mighty force in all instances of an elevated and heroic piety. It is one of Solomon's divine aphorisms, that " the path of the just is as the shining light, which shineth more and more unto the perfect day." By which, under the emblem of light, which from the fainter dawnings is continually increasing in brightness and warmth, till it has arrived at its meridian lustre, he gives us to understand the gradual progress of religion, or the divine life, in the souls of men; for, like the light, it is always ascending to greater heights, and never ceases improving in strength and vivacity, in purity and holiness, in love and devotion, in wisdom and experience, and in every Christian grace, till that Day—the everlasting day—the day of glory, which is indeed the " perfect Day," shall have begun to shine on the soul. And thus they who live the new life, do from small beginnings grow up by degrees unto perfection, proceed from step to step in the ways of godliness, until they have finished their course, and from babes in Christ become perfect men; " they forget those things that are behind, and reaching forth unto those things that are before, they press towards the mark;" and " beholding, as in a glass, the glory of the Lord, they are changed into the same image from glory to glory, as by the Spirit of the Lord."

THE HEAVENLY TENDENCY OF THE DIVINE LIFE.

It is observed of waters, that they can mount up as high as the source whence they flow. Just so, those "living waters," which form the noble principle of the new life, being derived from heaven, do, as our Saviour tells us, "spring up into life eternal;" and they in whose minds they dwell, "set no more their affections on things on earth, but on things above, where Christ sitteth on the right hand of God." Their great and sovereign end is to come to the enjoyment of God, and all other aims are in subserviency to this. It follows, that their conversation must be heavenly, that is, that they will demean themselves as the inhabitants of that other and better country, as citizens of the new Jerusalem, and denizens of heaven. This is the city to which they belong; to its privileges they have a right, and its customs and practices they endeavour to follow. Though they are in the world, yet they are not of the world, nor conform to it. They are guided by diviner maxims, and directed by nobler patterns; for, by conversing with their adorable Lord in pious thoughts and contemplations, they become acquainted with the manners of that happy place where he is, and they study to express them in their lives: so that their words and actions, and the whole of their behaviour, savour of heaven; and

1

even their very employments and callings, though they may seem to concern only the things of time, and though by men of worldly minds they are directed to no other end but the attaining of earth, and dross, and vanity; yet they improve them into opportunities of advancing heavenwards, and turn their incumbrances into spiritual advantages. And O how empty as well as insipid do the most alluring and delightful objects of this world appear to those happy souls that are thus powerfully attracted heavenwards!

This spiritual ascent of the soul is amongst the last and noblest efforts of the divine life here on earth, and shall hereafter be followed by a glorious and triumphant ascent of both soul and body, into the joys and felicities of the other world. As the Redeemer is ascended into heaven, so shall his true disciples likewise in due time. In that divine prayer wherewith he shuts up the gracious words which then proceeded out of his mouth, he makes it his request, that his peculiar people, that is, all true and sincere Christians, might be admitted into the heavenly mansions together with him, and there behold the luminous and transcendent majesty with which he is invested. " Father, I will that they whom thou hast given me, be with me where I am, that they may see my glory." And thus runs the joyful commission which he gave to Mary Magdalene, soon after his resurrection: " Go to my brethren, and say unto them, I ascend unto my Father and your Father, unto my God and

4

your God : " intimating, that as they were his brethren, and consequently had a peculiar interest in God, as their God and Father ; so they might ex pect, when qualified for it, to be advanced to the blissful vision and fruition of him, as he now was in his glorified humanity. Now, this will be partly fulfilled at death, when their souls being separated from these earthly tabernacles, shall be conveyed into the regions of rest and peace, there to enjoy the presence of the Lord ;—and—perfectly—at the great day, in which the dead in Christ being raised, they shall be caught up in the clouds to meet him in the air, and shall continue for ever in the perfect enjoy ment of the delights and glories of his everlasting kingdom.

FRUITS OF THE DIVINE LIFE.

Peace with God.

ONE of the glorious privileges for which the divine life qualifies, and to which it admits the soul, is, peace with God. The state of enmity is over, and that of reconciliation and friendship takes place; for, being " justified by faith, they have peace with God through Jesus Christ;" that is, being not only discharged from the guilt of sin, through the righteousness and merits of the Redeemer, but also cleansed from its defilement, by the purifying efficacies of his grace, they are restored to the favour of God, admitted into his special love, and become his peculiar friends and favourites. The distance is removed, peace proclaimed, and the parties amicably approach one another. There is a sweet interview between the blessed God and the truly justified. He sees his own image in them, and they see the source of their happiness in Him, and they dearly embrace one another, he with the arms of a fatherly, and they with a filial love. And as they have peace with God, so they have the peace of God, a peace whereof God is the immediate author, that sweet and ineffable serenity of spirit, arising from a certain and lively sense of being transformed by the renewing of the mind, and from the operative presence of the love and light of God, graciously manifesting himself in the inward man. This blessed peace is eternal life actually begun in the soul; it is the sweet foretaste of that fulness of joy, and those pure pleasures, that are at God's right hand, and in his presence for evermore. There is then true peace:—peace—in opposition to the spiritual disorders of our nature; for, in the state of unregeneracy, all our faculties and powers are lamentably out of order, and as it were dislocated, and it is only by regeneration that they can be set right again, and the soul restored, so far as can be consistent with this present life, to its primitive and harmonious state, which was a state of order and beauty, of health and soundness, and consequently of tranquillity and peace. There is also peace of conscience, a joyful freedom from the severe reproaches, the bitter reflections and cutting remorse, the anxious and restless feelings, that are always the attendants of sin, unless in those that are hardened through the deceitfulness of it, and so rendered insensible for a time. This is one of the glorious immunities of the regenerate, to be delivered from those overwhelming broils and tumults, which sin and guilt produce in the bosom of the sinner. For in them (I speak of the most advanced in goodness and virtue, the fathers and perfect men in Christ Jesus), in them, I say, a nobler principle, a diviner power, bears sway; for, " the law of the Spirit of life in Christ Jesus has made them free from the law of sin and death." The seed of God, that is, his divine grace and light, his holy inspirations and suggestions, his kind motions and mighty influences, this incorruptible seed remains in them, and springs up in their hearts, into all sorts of heavenly virtues, into good thoughts and pious inclinations, into righteousness, peace, and joy, and into a deep aversion and horror of sin, which they see in its native deformity, and know to be the great enemy of their happiness and of all their comforts, and consequently that they are bound by the most solemn ties, to keep at the greatest distance from it and from all the occasions that lead to it. And thus the Holy Spirit of God inhabiting the mind, and filling it with his peace and joy, is the certain proof that the divine grace dwells there. " For the Spirit himself beareth witness with our spirits, that we are the children of God."

HOPE OF GLORY.

ANOTHER privilege to which the divine life entitles is a lively hope, that is, a firm and well-grounded expectation of the glories of eternity, in the blissful presence and endless fruition of God. The first fruits give good grounds to hope for the full harvest, and the life of grace will infallibly issue in that of glory. " Blessed be the God and Father of our Lord Jesus Christ," said St. Peter in a divine rapture, " who according to his abundant mercy hath begotten us again unto a lively hope, by the resurrection of Christ from the dead, to an inheritance incorruptible, and undefiled, and that fadeth not away, reserved in heaven for us." The divine power and virtue of Christ's resurrection raises up into a new life, and the new life produces a lively hope, not a languid and ineffectual one, but a hope that prompts to a generous and operative piety, and inspires with the love of purity; for, as St. John tells us, " every man that hath this hope in him, purifieth himself even as he is pure." A soul that hopes for the undefiled inheritance, is sensible that he cannot have access to it without purity; and that to indulge sin and corruption in any measure, would weaken the confidence and cloud the joys of his hope. Whence it is evident, that a lively hope heightens the true Christian's aversion to sin, and guards him against those artifices of the enemy by which he endeavours to betray into the commission of it. It is for this reason that the great Apostle compares it to a helmet; for, as that piece of armour secures the head from wounds, so the hope of salvation, being opposed to the fiery darts of the devil, those violent temptations by which he attacks the hearts of the faithful, baffles and beats them back, without suffering them to do any harm.

Such is the power of a lively hope, that it keeps the soul firm and unmoveable, serene and composed in all states and conditions, so that nothing is able to shake its holy purposes, or disturb its repose. Hence, in the Epistle to the Hebrews, the Christian is said to " have this hope as an anchor of the soul both sure and steadfast, and which entereth into that within the veil." This similitude is a very significant one in many respects: for, as the anchor holds fast the ship and keeps it steady in the midst of storms and tempests; so in like manner the hope of glory stays and solaces the spirit of a Christian, keeps it firm and invincible, when tossed upon the waves, and exposed to the temptations of a troublesome world. Again, as the anchor rests not in the waters of the sea, but pierces through them, till it comes to the solid bottom; so likewise the grace of hope passes through all the shadowy and unstable

3

appearances of time, never fixing on any created thing, but continues its course till it enter into that within the veil, that is, into heaven, and there it finds its true object, even God himself, on whom it may rely with confidence and safety, and without any fear of disappointment. And indeed the prospect which hope gives the saints, both of the glories that are within the veil, and of their title to inherit them, is so very endearing that it must needs fill their hearts with joy unspeakable and glorious. "We rejoice in hope of the glory of God," said St. Paul. For what greater cause of rejoicing can we have, than the daily and well-grounded expectation of eternal life, especially since it is an expectation that will not disappoint us, " a hope that maketh not ashamed;" because, as the Apostle adds, " the love of God is shed abroad in our hearts, by the Holy Ghost given unto us."

'Tis true, did the saints only view their own nothingness and infirmities, it might, and not without reason, damp their hopes; but, on the other hand, when they consider the promises of God which are faithful and true ; when they consider the love of God which is infinite, and the power of his grace which is almighty; when they consider the merits of that dear Saviour that died for them, and ever liveth to make intercession for them, and that God, who sincerely wills their salvation, will refuse them nothing that is necessary to secure it; this supports their spirits, cherishes their hope, and

3

keeps them in a joyful elevation and sweet serenity. The first fruits give good grounds to hope for the full harvest, and the life of grace must issue in that of glory. Blessed be the God and Father of our Lord Jesus Christ, who according to his abundant mercy hath begotten us again into a lively hope, by the resurrection of Christ from the dead; to an inheritance incorruptible and undefiled, and that fadeth not away, reserved in heaven for us.

THE END.

www.ingramcontent.com/pod-product-compliance
Lightning Source LLC
LaVergne TN
LVHW081346060426
835508LV00017B/1437